MAXIMUM POINTS – MINIMUM PANIC

THE ESSENTIAL GUIDE TO SURVIVING EXAMS

KEVIN FLANAGAN

First published in 1996 by
Marino Books
An imprint of Mercier Press
16 Hume Street Dublin 2

Trade enquiries to Mercier Press
PO Box 5, 5 French Church Street, Cork

A Marino Original

© Kevin Flanagan 1996

ISBN 1 86023 138 5

10 9 8 7 6 5 4 3 2 1

A CIP record for this title is available from the British Library

Cover design by Cathy Dineen
Set by Richard Parfrey
Printed in Ireland by ColourBooks,
Baldoyle Industrial Estate, Dublin 13

This book is sold subject to the condition that it shall not, by way of trade or otherwise, be lent, resold, hired out or otherwise circulated without the publisher's prior consent in any form of binding or cover other than that in which it is published and without a similar condition including this condition being imposed on the subsequent purchaser.

No part of this publication may be reproduced or transmitted in any form or by any means, electronic or mechanical, including photocopying, recording or any information or retrieval system, without the prior permission of the publisher in writing.

WHAT OTHERS HAVE TO SAY . . .

Modern research shows that stress influences virtually every area of life, often negatively. I think Kevin's ideas will be particularly useful in helping students develop lifelong skills in handling stress.
Maria Murphy, Researcher, Cardio-Rehabilitation Unit, Beaumont Hospital

I have worked with Kevin professionally for many years and have seen him prepare hundreds of students for stressful exams. His techniques are spot on!
Glenda Chop, NCEF Course Coordinator, Dublin

Kevin presents PEAI Stress Management workshops to physical education teachers which are valuable and practical to the teachers and their students alike.
Gráinne O'Donovan, Chief Administrator, PEAI, University of Limerick

Every day I come across cases of students suffering from exam stress. This book, I feel, offers practical solutions to this problem and will be invaluable to students and parents alike.
Breandán Ó Murchú, Vice Principal, Willow Park School, Dublin

ABOUT THE AUTHOR

Kevin Flanagan was principal of the NCEF course at Litton Lane Studios in Dublin. He served on the NCEF Review Committee and Examination Board. He is now director of the Stress Clinic in Dublin and a focusing facilitator, having completed certification with Professor Gendlin at the Focusing Institute in Chicago. Kevin writes regularly on stress for the media and is currently completing his second book.

DEDICATION

To Alan, the best of friends at all times, and the Marines. To Ciarán, who makes my heart sing. To Mairéad. To Phil and Cathleen for starting me on my journey and to Pete, Ed and Gene for showing me how to get there.

To Paul, Spen, Phil, Peter and Mary for being friends all along and all at Litton Lane – thanks for the help!

To Pat for keeping the show on the road and Gerry Kean for all his help and friendship.

Finally to the inner truth that comes when you listen to the quiet, still voice inside.

ACKNOWLEDGEMENTS

My thanks are due to Jo and Anne for their enthusiastic support, to Claire for typing the manuscript in record time and Proinsias Ó Conluain for proofreading, to Niamh, Nuala, Glenda and Lisa at Litton Lane for their help and care. Also to Mum for her ideas, to all at the NCEF, especially Mary and Louise, and the PEAI, especially Gráinne. Working with them has opened my eyes. To Susan Madigan for her graphics and Cathy Dineen for the cover and inside cartoons. Thanks to all at the Berkeley Library at Trinity College, Dublin for the use of the wonderful facilities and all the staff at Fitzers, the Shelbourne and Blazing Saddles for keeping me going with food and drink while writing! To all at Johnston Print for their support over the years. Finally to all the people I have worked with in focusing, and all my past NCEF and ITEC students. Seeing their efforts and struggles to improve and educate themselves inspired this book.

Kevin Flanagan
Dublin 1996

CONTENTS

1	Why I Wrote This Book	9
2	Introduction	11
3	What is 'Exam Stress' and Why Does it Affect me?	15
4	The Stress Test	26
5	Looking after My Body	30
	Burnout and Breakdown	32
	Exercise Away Stress	35
	How to Sleep Deeply and Learn at the Same Time	39
	Feeding My Brain – How to Eat to Learn	47
	The Power Snooze	54
	Worry and How to Deal with It	55
	Love Yourself	57
6	How To Pass Exams – a Personal Guide	59
	How the Brain Works	59
	How Can I Map Out My Notes	63
	The Six-Step Revision Plan	68
	Disadvantages of Cramming	71
	How Can I Make My Homework Easier and More Effective?	71
	Study Distractions – the 'Hit List'	77
	Study Tips – How To Be More Effective in Less Time	83
	Use Your Friends To Help You To Pass Exams	87

	Surface Learning/Deep Learning	92
7	Countdown to Judgement Day	96
	Phase I: the Pre-Mock Period	97
	Phase II: The Mock Exams	98
	Phase III: Period Between Mocks and Real Exams	99
	Phase IV: Four Weeks to Go	100
	D-Day	103
	After the Exams	109
8	Is There Life After Exams?	111
	Whose Life Is It Anyway?	112
	Further Reading	122
	Further Information	123
	Repeat Stress Test	124

1

WHY I WROTE THIS BOOK

In December 1995 a report on stress in schools was presented by Eithne Fitzgerald, Minister for Labour, to the Minister for Education, Niamh Bhreathnach. The survey was carried out among 26,161 staff and 458,372 pupils at both primary and post-primary schools in the academic year 1993-4.

It showed that out of the 12,473 workdays lost more than 6,000 were lost due to stress – nearly 50 per cent. In fact stress accounted for 55 per cent of days lost in post-primary schools. The report's recommendations included the following:

- It should be recognised that pressure can trigger stress-related illness.
- This illness should be taken seriously and not dismissed as weakness.
- A supportive culture should be developed to help those suffering from stress.
- Training should be given in coping techniques.

I have been working in the area of stress for nearly a decade and am convinced of the need for such a book as this. It is a manual that can be used by students facing the stress of exams as well as their teachers and parents. It can be supplemented by the audio cassette *Maximum Points - Minimum Panic,* which provides direct experiential help in such areas as motivation, effective study, deep learning, relaxation, comfortable sleep and sleep learning. The book and tape offer a holistic approach, providing additional advice and guidance on such matters as diet, exercise, time management, resolution of worry, problems of motivation and the unique stress of doing exams.

For the past ten years I have been involved in preparing students for the National Certificate in Exercise and Fitness examinations. I was involved from the beginning of the scheme and worked with my colleagues to make it what it is today - the national training scheme for fitness instructors in Ireland, awarded jointly by the University of Limerick and the Physical Education Association of Ireland (PEAI).

During that time we were trying to design an examination system that was both fair and practical - it was, after all, preparing people for jobs in the growing fitness industry. The course catered not just for school leavers but for mature students who had sometimes been out of the exam system for twenty or thirty years. My experience of coaching these vulnerable people through practical and written exams and continuous assessment is the basis of this book. In ten years I came to realise that people can, with a little help, face up to the difficulties and stresses of the exam system, even though these have grown very considerably.

I hope this book and the experience it shares will help students to pass along this often rocky and difficult road and come out the other side stronger and with the unique sense of achievement that passing exams can give. To you I say: use this book as a guide and a coach, picking through the various sections as you need them. I wish you all the best on your journey. If you need particular help you can write to me at the address at the back of the book. Good luck!

2

INTRODUCTION

THE TRUE STORY OF THE RABBIT

Picture the scene: a large laboratory in America where experiments were carried out on animals. In this particular experiment hundreds of rabbits were fed cancer-forming toxins, in order to determine how long it took for them to develop tumours and die. The rabbits were kept individually in hundreds of small hutches which stretched from ground level right up to the ceiling many metres above.

During the experiment the researchers began to notice something very strange. The rabbits on the lowest levels were all surviving while those higher up were not. The scientists tested the air, water and temperature to see if there was a difference at ground level but they could find nothing. It was only by accident that they eventually discovered the reason. The laboratory technician who looked after this particular group of rabbits used a ladder while cleaning out the higher hutches. He'd balance the food tray on his arm while he changed the water and swept out the droppings. But when he got off the ladder to attend to the hutches at floor level he had both hands free and after cleaning and feeding the rabbits he did one extra thing that made all the difference. He picked up each rabbit and spent a few moments cuddling and playing with it. He even had a pet name for them all and would coo and stroke them affectionately. It seemed that this single act of daily kindness kept these rabbits alive and well

I believe this teaches us something about taking care of ourselves. You are probably reading this book because you are about to undergo a major examination. Nowadays that is a stressful business. Examinations promote a sense of isolation and pressure on individuals who feel they are under the microscope in an unenviable way. Does this remind you of anything? If you don't want to end up like the neglected rabbits – burnt-out, exhausted or worse – it is important to look after yourself; the pressure to succeed can do you a great deal of damage.

YOUR FRIEND – YOUR COACH

I hope this book and the accompanying tape will act as friend and coach to you in the quest to succeed in your examinations. As a friend I hope to give you support and reassurance in your long and often difficult journey; as your coach I hope to advise and guide you so that you will achieve your maximum points with minimum panic. The advice is based on experience and the latest research. Follow it and not only will you do well; you will learn how to perform better in all areas of your life: planning your time, eating well, exercising, learning how to get the most out of your life while dealing with stress.

YOUR UNIQUENESS

Remember you are unique: the most important thing you can ever learn is the unique contribution you can make to life. This may not necessarily be what your parents and teachers have planned for you. But there was no school

examination that prepared Bob Geldof, Dolores O'Riordan, Bono, Neil Jordan, Gillian Bowler, Phil Babb, Sinéad O'Connor, Sean Hughes, Ken Doherty, President Mary Robinson, Roddy Doyle or Paul McGuinness for their unique careers. And if they had continued to work in the jobs they were first advised to take up we would all be the poorer for it.

So let us begin and get ready to meet one of the first big hurdles in life – the school examination system. Together we can jump that hurdle successfully and who knows where you can go from there. The world is your oyster!

HOW TO USE THIS BOOK

Pick and choose. You don't have to read this book from cover to cover. It is rather like the 'pick'n'mix' sweet counters you find at cinemas nowadays where you take what you want – a few of these, a lot of those. Keep this book with you and use it whenever you need it. Listen to the tape as often as you like; it will help you to relax, learn subconsciously, sleep well and concentrate fully. It will also bring out your hidden unconscious creativity. Come back to the book as often as you like. There are no rules except the ones you choose to make.

3

WHAT IS EXAM STRESS AND WHY DOES IT AFFECT ME?

I'M NOT JUST A MIND – I'M A BODY AS WELL!

The problem with our exam system is that it puts a lot of emphasis on the performance of the brain and on particular functions of the brain at that: the cognitive, analytic, mathematical, logical and rational functions. There are two big problems with this approach. The first is that these particular functions are only some of many that the brain can perform. (To find out more see the section 'How My Brain Works'.) The other main difficulty of our exam system is that it emphasises brain performance at the expense of the body's performance and capabilities. Ever notice that there is no school-leaving examination in rugby, hockey, swimming, aerobics or disco dancing – all things that people will do during their adult life long after they have given up thinking about geometry or physics.

Neither are there exams in such skills as how to exercise properly and get the best performance out of your body or even how to prevent disease and look after your body in its old age – things you will need to do long after you have stopped thinking about fractions or the biology of frogs. And have you noticed that we are not always coached at school in the most vital of physical skills, one that can save lives, namely First Aid and cardio-pulmonary resuscitation – dealing with heart attacks or other life-threatening events such as epileptic fits, to say nothing of cuts, wounds and accidents of all sorts. It is incredible to think that nearly all young adults are equipped to deal with abstract mental equations while they would be at a terrifying loss if someone suffered a heart attack in their presence.

OUR BODY – OUR HOME

The truth is that the examination system over-emphasises the mind at the expense of the body, so much so that students lose touch with their body's feelings and needs and ignore the vital signs that it sends out when it requires rest, sleep and play. This is a dangerous, for the mind cannot operate without the body. Try writing an hour-long essay while holding your breath! Yet we often ignore the body's pleas for rest and change. We punish it remorselessly, pushing it to its limits and beyond. Then we curse it when it becomes sick and exhausted and lets us down.

This is exam stress. It is not a case of the body's letting us down but rather of our letting the body down. Your body is always on your side and it is designed to help you to perform to your maximum. But it does need rest.

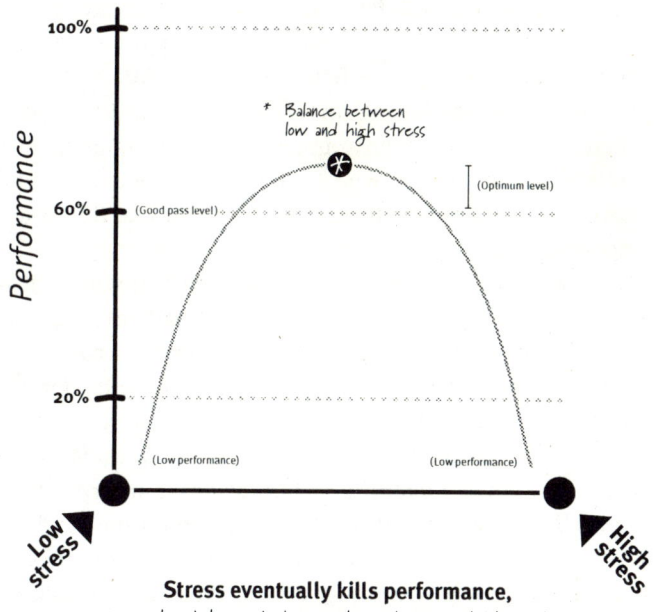

THE MAD AXEMAN – A STORY FOR OUR TIME

A young man called Seán emigrated to Canada. He was physically strong and determined to succeed, and he'd always had an ambition to be a lumberjack. He eventually got his first job and the boss gave him his own axe and a sharpening stone and the following advice: 'Keep your axe sharp and cut me down twenty trees a day and within two years you will be a rich man.'

Well Seán was nothing if not enthusiastic. The first day he cut down ten trees, the next day twelve, and by the end of the week he'd felled twenty trees in the day. But he was not content with that. As his technique improved the daily number of trees he felled increased. By the end of the month he was felling forty trees a day and making a small fortune. The older lumberjacks took him aside and advised him to slow down. 'Take time out; relax, spend a morning sharpening your axe. If you go on like this you'll burn yourself out.'

But youth is headstrong and Seán was convinced he'd have his fortune made in half the time if he kept it up. For a while it worked; then things started slipping. From forty trees a day he was soon down to thirty, then twenty. Finally by the third month he was barely making ten while actually working harder than ever before. He could not understand it. His workmates again took him aside. 'You are killing yourself, my friend; you must spend some time resting.' But Seán would not listen. Instead he redoubled his efforts, getting up even earlier and working even later, attacking the trees with a venom that was terrifying. But the more he attacked the fewer trees fell. Eventually he spent a whole day attacking a single tree. By sunset it was still standing and Seán fell in a heap on the ground, sobbing and cursing the tree, life and fate itself. He could not understand what was happening to him and why the tree refused to fall even

after hours of attacking it. He felt a failure, decided to quit and approached the boss with a sense of despair. The boss was angry with him. 'What do you expect if you don't put in the work!'

'But I have never worked harder,' complained Seán. 'I get up two hours before the others. I work an hour after they have all gone home. But it just doesn't happen any more. The trees won't fall.' The boss nodded sarcastically. It was only when Seán handed back his axe and sharpening stone that the penny dropped. The boss looked at his axe in disbelief. 'This axe is totally blunt. It could not cut down a matchstick, let alone a tree!' Then he took up the sharpening stone. It was as smooth and round as the day he'd handed it over. The boss looked sharply at Seán. 'Did you ever use this on your axe?' Seán shook his head. 'When would I have had the time to use that. I was too busy trying to cut down those damned trees!'

THE STORY OF MODERN-DAY STRESS

The story of Seán is the story of our time. Do you ever take time to sharpen your axe? Do you ever take time out to recuperate? Or do you work even longer hours with even poorer results? The truth is that we need to rest our bodies. If we don't, they become blunt and ineffective. It doesn't matter how long we work – our efforts will still be ineffective and in the end a waste of precious time.

CAN YOU CUT DOWN A TREE WITH A BLUNT AXE?

HOW WILL THIS BOOK & TAPE HELP ME?

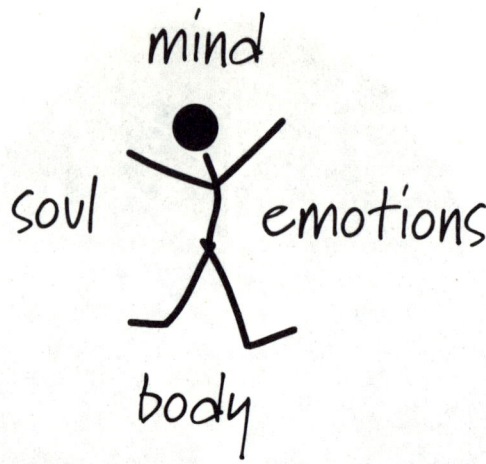

Mind
It will help me to look after my mind – helping it to learn, analyse, revise, think under pressure and be creative.

Emotions
It will help me to acknowledge strong emotions like fear and doubt and find motivation deep inside myself.

Soul
It will help me to find my own unique goal in life and the ways I can uniquely contribute to the universe.

Body
It will help me to look after my health by eating, drinking, sleeping and exercising well.

WHY DO EXAMS CAUSE STRESS?

Picture this: You wake up in the morning, jump out of bed with a squeal of delight and run out the door full of the joys of life. 'Sorry Mum,' you call back merrily. 'I'm too excited to eat breakfast – my first exam is this morning and I just can't wait to get at the paper. I'll see you later.' And as you skip down the road you look up with tears of joy in your eyes and say breathlessly, 'Thank you, God, for giving me my exams.'

Doesn't fit, does it And why is that? It's simple, really. Exams represent a threat to us. They trigger the same ancient survival instinct as when our ancestors were attacked by the sabre-toothed tiger or a hostile tribe intent on rape and murder. That response was originally to save us from death or life-threatening injury; it's still with us and it's called the fight or flight response.

FIGHT OR FLIGHT RESPONSE

The body reacts automatically once it detects a threat – or what it has been conditioned to see as a threat. This is important as the body can be conditioned or trained into thinking that anything is a life-endangering threat, including exams – which clearly aren't in the same league as a rampaging tiger. The good thing about this response is that it can also be trained not to see things as a threat, including exams – but we'll be working on that later

Your body detects a threat and automatically several things happen at once. Just put a tick beside the things you've noticed happening to you when you think about or approach your exams. You will soon find out if you are suffering exam stress.

Effects of 'Fight or Flight' Instinct	Reason for Instinct
Heart beats faster	To pump more blood to working muscles
Adrenaline & cortisol flood body	To heighten awareness – it wakes you up to 'fight or flight'
Perspiration	To cool down body while it fights or flees
Breathing quickens	To increase oxygen supply to help it fight or flee
Agent that clots blood floods body	Stops you bleeding to death if injured
Fat and sugars pour into bloodstream	Provide instant energy to fight or flee
Pupils dilate (open wide)	Let in more light in order to fight or flee more efficiently
Muscles tense, causing hair to stand 'on end'	Preparing the body to take a blow or strike back

How It Affects Us Nowadays	Tick
Feeling of heart pounding in chest	☐
Nervousness and 'butterflies-in-tummy' feeling	☐
Sweaty palms, forehead, back	☐
Shortness of breath, difficulty in breathing	☐
Silent killer leading to heart attack	☐
Agitation and nervousness, pent-up energy, feeling 'on edge'	☐
Staring, frightened eyes, look of someone under attack	☐
Stiff shoulder, neck – feeling you're about to lash out at something	☐

4

STRESS TEST

HOW STRESSED AM I?

While exams may not threaten our physical wellbeing directly they do threaten our sense of self-esteem, our reputation and our value in the eyes of others. Taken to an extreme, the fear of facing exams can even undermine and destroy our health – and our lives.

This short test will give you an idea how stressed you are, how much you are suffering from the fight or flight response.

Directions
Simply put a cross where you think you are on the graph. Don't think about it too long. Then join up the xs. This will give you a clear idea of where you are on the scale. 0 = little or no stress. 10 = dangerous or extreme stress. At the end of this book is an identical chart. Fill it in when you have put into practice the guidelines outlined in this book and see if there's a difference. There should be if you give them time to work.

BODY

Relaxed	0 1 2 3 4 5 6 7 8 9 10	Extreme Stress
Steady heartbeat	. . . .	Palpitations
Calm relaxed feelings	. . . .	'On edge' feelings
Dry hands and brow	. . . .	Clammy hands and brow
Slow steady breathing	. . . .	Fast breathing, shortness of breath
Steady hand, relaxed muscles	. . . .	Shaking hand, tensed muscles, stiff neck or shoulders
Steady flow of energy; don't get tired easily	. . . .	Sudden 'bursts' of frantic energy followed by exhaustion, extreme tiredness
Sleep like a log	. . . .	Can't sleep at all
Eat well regularly	. . . .	Can't eat at all or binge
Digest food easily	. . . .	Can't digest food at all
Skin, hair and eyes bright and healthy	. . . .	Skin, hair and eyes dull or blotchy

MIND

Relaxed	0 1 2 4 5 6 7 8 9 10	**Extreme Stress**
Can make decisions and stick with them	. . . .	Can't make decisions or keep changing mind
Can calculate and see all sides of a problem	. . . .	Can't calculate or see what the problem is at all
Can work long hours doing 'brain' work	. . . .	Can't do any 'brain' work at all

EMOTIONS

Relaxed	0 1 2 4 5 6 7 8 9 10	Extreme Stress
Steady, reliable mood	. . . .	Extreme mood swings
Sense of feeling 'good' about life	. . . .	Depression or feeling 'bad' about life
Feeling 'I can cope'	. . . .	Feeling 'I can't cope'
Feeling loved by family	. . . .	Feeling unloved by family
Feeling supported by friends	. . . .	Feeling 'I have no friends'

SOUL

Relaxed	0 1 2 4 5 6 7 8 9 10	Extreme Stress
Feeling I'm worth a lot	. . . .	Feeling I'm worth nothing
Feeling life is definitely worth living	. . . .	Feeling life is not worth living
Feeling I am loved by people and/or a higher power	. . . .	Feeling unloved by people and/or a higher power
Feeling my life has a a purpose	. . . .	Feeling my life is purposeless
Feeling there is love and protection in the world	. . . .	Feeling threatened and vulnerable
Feeling I have a part to play in life	. . . .	Feeling I have no part part to play in life at all

5

LOOKING AFTER MY BODY

IT'S NOT ALL IN THE MIND

Modern society reflects the anxieties generated by what we may call the 'points' mentality. This mentality results from students considering themselves a success only if they achieve the right number of points, even though his is something that is outside themselves and has nothing to do with whether they are intrinsically good or decent human beings. Failing to get these vital points can often be the result of bad luck or PMT. Other factors are: 'How well off are my parents?' or 'Do I happen to live in the right area, come from the right socio-economic background or go to the "right" school?'

In the end society as a whole (and that means you and me) needs urgently to address the problem of how we educate ourselves and the social consequences of our educational system. Otherwise we run the risk of suffering seriously from the results of stress and the frantic need to achieve at all costs.

But back to our bodies. How can we look after our bodies so that our minds can function at their best?

Untreated stress
leads to burnout and breakdown

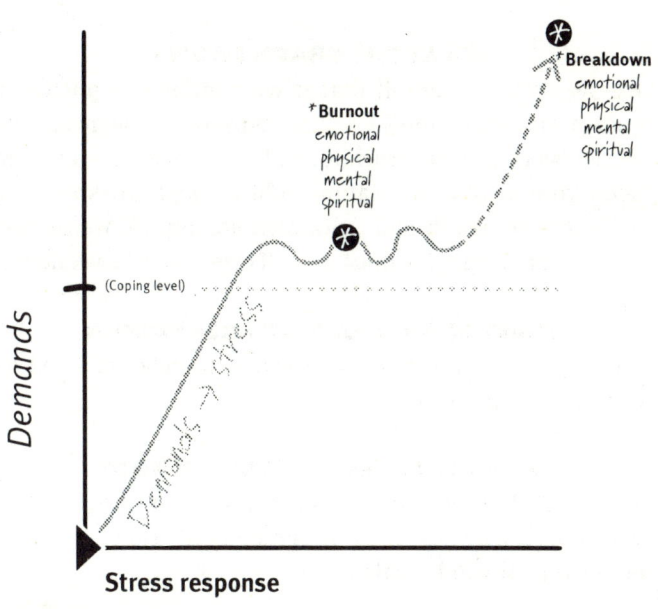

BURNOUT AND BREAKDOWN

The story of the Mad Axeman shows us that if we push our bodies too far they will:

- Become less effective
- Become exhausted
- Become ill
- Break down

usually in that order. In fact, the evidence shows that the longer we work the less effective we become.

WHAT THE GRAPH SHOWS
We see from the graph that if we continue to push our bodies without taking a break we burn out. This means we work less effectively. Burnout will affect every area of our lives from mental calculation right through to aspects of our physical health and emotional stability. If we do not take action during burnout we will eventually break down.

SIGNS OF BURNOUT OR BREAKDOWN
Thediagram on the next page shows the classic signs of burnout/breakdown.

MY BRAIN NEEDS A HEALTHY BODY
Your body literally carries your brain on its shoulders. If you look after your body your mind will function more effectively. It will be able to:

- study better
- think more clearly for longer
- take the pressure of exams more in its stride
- achieve better exam results

SIGNS OF BURNOUT

Mental

Difficulty in calculating, concentrating, studying, making decisions; experiencing headaches, sleep problems

Spiritual

Tired and frustrated with 'life', problems with motivation and losing interest in things, a 'what's the point?' feeling

Emotional

Mood swings, emotional outbursts, extreme nervousness and tiredness, comfort 'addictions'

Physical

Exhaustion, frequent illness like colds, flus and difficulty in getting rid of them, eating disorders, stiff shoulders, tension headaches

Warning: If you do not do something about burnout it will develop into a breakdown, which is far more serious and for which you may need professional help.

SIGNS OF BREAKDOWN

Mental

Inability to think, plan, decide, study; sense of coming to a standstill or dead end

Spiritual

Despair, hopelessness, 'breaking of the spirit' and interest in life. Withdrawal and isolation; in extreme cases suicide

Emotional

Inability to deal with pressure, demands, deadlines, relationships

Physical

Breakdown in health often accompanied by serious illness that does not respond to treatment

Just look at how poorly you perform when you are tired, stressed out and sleeping badly. Let's look at simple ways to help your body to perform to its maximum.

EXERCISE AWAY STRESS

Running will literally get rid of all the chemicals that flood the body when we are stressed. Exercise also produces hormones called endorphins which give a natural sense of wellbeing. Ever gone out for a brisk walk or run feeling stressed and come back feeling glowing and warm, your cares forgotten? That is the endorphin effect of exercise and it happens every time you take exercise. Endorphin has effects as powerful as popularly prescribed tranquilisers, but unlike tranquillisers:

- has no toxic side effects
- is non-addictive
- allows the correct dose to go straight to the part of the brain that needs it, allowing other activities like driving to go on unaffected
- in an emergency causes the brain to produce a natural antidote that removes the endorphin almost instantly, allowing the individual to respond fully to the crisis.

The fact is that our bodies can be our own best pharmacy and doctor, prescribing the right drug and delivering it to the correct part of the body. All this can occur quite naturally, with no need for prescriptions, doctors' visits or hospital fees. Your body is, in fact, a walking medical miracle.

WHAT SORT OF EXERCISE SHOULD I TAKE?

WALKING

Probably the cheapest, easiest and best exercise available. All you need is a pair of shoes – there's plenty of road out there.

How often? The recommendation of the American College of Sports Medicine, arrived at after years of research, is a half-hour daily walk or a one-hour walk every second day. The advantage of walking is that it can be done at any time without elaborate preparations. It can become part of your daily schedule, e.g. walking to school or college instead of taking the bus.

JOGGING

While walking gets you healthy, jogging or running will get you fit, especially aerobically fit. This has the advantage of giving you added endurance – a component of fitness that will help you to study longer and cope with stress more effectively. It will also help you to eat, sleep and relax. But you will need to invest in a good pair of running shoes and a tracksuit.

How often? A half-hour jog every other day is recommended.

CYCLING

Like jogging, cycling is a great form of exercise but you do need to get a bike. Traffic and poor weather can make it more problematic than walking.

How often? A half-hour daily or one hour every other day. Try to avoid traffic and pollution.

I AM my own Doctor, Chemist & Hospital.

SWIMMING

Great exercise but not everyone has access to a pool. The advantage is that there is less strain on the joints than with running.

How often? Half an hour to an hour every other day.

SPORT

The 'fighting' response to stress. Here you can literally take out your aggression on a ball or opponent – which some people find more satisfying than just running. Make sure you are on a fitness training programme as part of your sport. It can be dangerous to engage in sports, especially contact sports like football or rugby if you are unfit and not properly warmed up.

How often? With training sessions you should aim to be out pursuing your sport three to five times per week.

A SALUTARY WARNING – IT'S A DOG'S LIFE!

Imagine that you had a pet dog and all you did with it each day was take it on the bus with you in the morning, make it sit by your side during classes all day, come home on the bus in the evening and stay in all night while you studied or watched television. How would the dog feel after a week of this? How would it feel after a month without a run in the park or chase down the road? It would probably be on tranquillisers! Well, humans have the same need for exercise. At the bottom of it we are animals also and if we don't exercise we become like animals in captivity – depressed. The problem is that human beings choose their own captivity and lack of exercise. In fact eight out of ten adults do not exercise at all Is it any wonder we are all stressed out, overweight and unhealthy. Go on . . . exercise daily and you will enjoy the following benefits:

- better sleep
- improved weight control
- more stamina and endurance
- improved concentration
- more effective study
- less stress
- the endorphin 'high' – a natural state of wellbeing and exhilaration that comes after exercise

Regular exercise will also dramatically improve your ability to cope with exam stress. Your overall results and prospects will improve if you make exercise a part of your weekly routine.

HOW TO SLEEP DEEPLY AND LEARN AT THE SAME TIME

In the 1960s and 1970s the Russians and their Eastern European neighbours made huge strides in athletic achievements. It is only now, after the fall of communism, that we are learning just how much 'sleep' training was used by the top coaches to help their protégés perform to their maximum. Coaches in the west have since developed many of these techniques and now you too can use some of them to help to maximise your learning potential while sleeping. The obvious advantage is that the technique requires no conscious effort from you. You simply go to sleep and let your unconscious go to work for you. Sounds too good to be true? Not at all, The research is now comprehensive and we can put together a package that will help you to sleep well and improve your learning *at the same time.*

STEP 1: TAKE EXERCISE

Exercise regularly and take a walk during the evening. This will help the body to become naturally tired and ready for sleep. Exercise helps the muscles to stretch and relax, which also helps sleep.

STEP 2: AVOID EATING

Avoid eating late. Food and drink are energy sources which, if not burnt off, can keep you awake. In particular, sugary snacks and drinks can give you an energy surge that will keep you awake. Caffeine, which is found in coffee, tea and soft drinks, has the same effect. Take a hot milky drink. Milk contains a substance that helps to promote sleep naturally.

STEP 3: PLAN YOUR DAY

Write out your schedule for tomorrow if you haven't already done so. This will stop the mind worrying about what it has to do. Besides, writing down tomorrow's tasks allows the problem-solving part of the sleep cycle unconsciously to work on things you may be concerned with – hence the old saying 'to sleep on it'.

Use an A and B Priorities List:

A List – Things I have to do tomorrow

B List – Things I'd like to do tomorrow

The problem with many people is that they are very good at completing the B list while causing themselves stress by leaving the A list things undone.

SPECIAL TIP: DO THE UNPLEASANT THINGS FIRST

One of the most successful businessmen in America, Henry Ford II, is said to have based his success on the following formula. Do unpleasant tasks *early in the day*. If Henry had to fire someone he would never put it off until the afternoon. Rather he would aim to have all his unpleasant tasks done by 9 am. That way they would not be on his mind for the rest of the day. Try the same approach yourself. You know that nasty piece of revision or that essay that's late or that project you've been putting off. Why not try getting all or part of it done as early as possible in the day? Think how you will feel when it's done. And in your personal life you can try the same thing. Remember those bad marks you avoided telling your parents about or that friend you need to apologise to. Try doing such tasks first thing in the morning and see how you feel.

Here is a sample A and B list.

A – *Have to do*s	B – *Like to do*s
e.g.	
Finish English essay – another 2,000 words	Catch MTV's *Unplugged*
Revise French verbs p. 127	Visit Susan
Read Chapter 4 of *A Portrait of the Artist*	Borrow and listen to John's new CD
Hour training session with team	*Destruction Derby* video game
Take half-hour walk	

Now fill in your own agenda for tomorrow. Cover all areas of your life, putting the most important things first.

My Own As for tomorrow   *My Own Bs for tomorrow*

_____   _____

_____   _____

_____   _____

_____   _____

_____   _____

STEP 4: HAVE A RELAXING BATH

Have a bath. You can also use essential oils – the oils made up only of crushed natural flowers – in the water. Lavender is especially good for relaxing and is available in any pharmacy or health food store. You can also light a candle and play soothing music. Your body will soon begin to relax.

STEP 5: MSKE YOUR BEDROOM WARM AND RELAXING

Turn your bedroom into a warm relaxing environment. This can be easily done. Light a candle, burn essential oils like lavender in one of the oil burners you can buy in any health shop. Play relaxing music softly in the background. Make sure your bed is warm. Use a hot-water bottle. Tell people you are retiring and don't want to be disturbed.

STEP 6: RELAX YOUR MUSCLES

Tighten then relax your muscles. Start with the eyes. Squeeze them tightly shut for a second, then allow them to relax. Take a deep breath and notice how it feels to let your eyes relax. Then when they feel warm and relaxed move on to the jaw. Clench your teeth for a second and then relax the jaw. Take a deep breath and just enjoy the sensation of feeling your jaw heavy and relaxed. Continue this exercise, tightening and releasing the muscles of the following parts of the body:

- neck
- shoulders
- arms
- fist
- stomach
- hips
- thighs
- calves
- feet

STEP 7: USE A TAPE

Use a tape designed to help you relax, sleep and learn. The *Maximum Points – Minimum Panic* audio tape that accompanies this book is specially designed to do just that and is available in bookshops. It will help the body to sleep while encouraging the unconscious to process all the material you have learnt during the day. It will also encourage the mind to problem-solve while sleeping – an activity that occurs naturally in part of the sleeping cycle.

Tapes like this are very useful in that they do the work for you. All you do is slip on the headphones or put on the tape before going to sleep. Your conscious and unconscious mind do the rest for you.

STEP 8: DOING REVISION – MAPPING THE MAIN THINGS LEARNT

Take a few minutes, no more than five or six, to list the main things you learned that day. To help, draw a simple map like the biology one below and list off the key headings that you covered, but no more than that. Research shows that proper revision will keep you in touch with up to 90 per cent of the knowledge that would otherwise be lost. Using key words opens something rather like a computer file in your head and allows retrieval of the rest of the information from memory. Do a small map of each of the subjects you cover each day – it will take only a couple of minutes once you get the hang of it.

Doing this sort of effective revision also makes you feel good. Your conscious and unconscious mind see the effort you are making and you will be rewarded with the gratifying feeling of being on top of things. It also brings the study material of the day up to the surface and ready for the next step.

STEP 9: LEARN WHILE YOU SLEEP

After you have recalled all the main information of the day and written it down in simple 'mind-map' form, turn off your light and make yourself comfortable and ready for sleep. Let the mind-maps you have just drawn swim back into focus as you close your eyes ready for sleep. Imagine the shape of the map. Note the main heading and the smaller sub-headings. If these are written or underlined in different colours it will help you to picture them. Just let your unconscious memory throw the mind-maps up on your inner mental screen. Let it do the work for you. With a little practice you'll be amazed how easily it works.

Finally, invite the mind to absorb and recall the 'maps' while you sleep during the night. Invite your unconscious

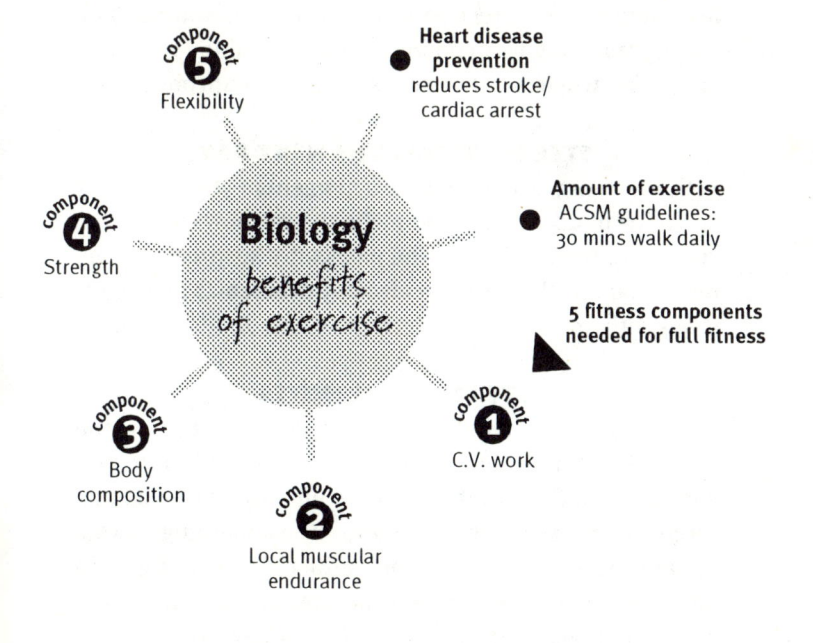

Biology
benefits of exercise

- **component 5** Flexibility
- **component 4** Strength
- **component 3** Body composition
- **component 2** Local muscular endurance
- **component 1** C.V. work

Biology benefits of exercise

- **Heart disease prevention** reduces stroke/cardiac arrest
- **Amount of exercise** ACSM guidelines: 30 mins walk daily
- **5 fitness components needed for full fitness**

creativity to problem-solve for you while you sleep, working on any unresolved problem you may have. It is now known that the unconscious responds to such invitations, especially if they are couched in this open, friendly way. Research at the University of Chicago has further shown that the unconscious really works for our best interests and will offer solutions to our problems. We only have to ask. The research also shows that during sleep answers can come symbolically in the form of dreams and intuitive insights. You will be amazed at how effectively you will begin to memorise information and solve your study and other personal problems. And with all this comes an improvement in self-confidence and self-belief and a lessening of exam-related stress. After all, you are now doing something very concrete about your study workload, and stress will lessen both consciously and unconsciously.

STEP 10: RECALL THE NEXT DAY

In the morning, when you have a moment to yourself, recall again the mind-maps of last night and see how clearly they come into focus. You may be pleasantly surprised at how much you recall. Check out also any problems you went to sleep with and see if they feel any closer to resolution.

STEP 11: MAKE NOTES

Finally, keep a small notebook and jot down any dreams or insights that come to you. (You may find it best to note your dreams the minute you wake up; otherwise you may forget them.) See if the dream matches anything in your life at the moment: a worry or conflict. See if it offers any new angle on it or a path to resolution. If it doesn't offer a solution immediately it may do in a few days' time – that's why it's important to keep a record of it.

FINAL THOUGHT

Try out these tips for learning while sleeping and you could be in for a very pleasant surprise. Your learning should markedly improve over time and you may receive valuable insights from your dreams and intuition. Finally – sweet dreams! You deserve them!

Alternatively, use the *Maximum Points – Minimum Panic* audio tape and this will do the work for you. Simply slip it into your Walkman or tape machine and lie back, ready for sleep. The 'Learn While You Rest' section will take you through a complete relaxation and learning session. It will help the body to sleep while encouraging the unconscious to process all the material you have learnt during the day. To a background of harmonious music and gentle waves lapping the seashore you will be guided on a wonderful journey that will end in deep restful sleep. The learning and creative problem-solving will continue through the night. Side 1 of the tape includes a summary of the key points of this book and will remind you of the simple steps necessary to achieve 'maximum points' with 'minimum panic' (See the back of this book for order form).

FEEDING MY BRAIN – HOW TO EAT TO LEARN

A couple of years ago a research study was published in the United Kingdom about nutrition and its relation to children's academic performance. The report concluded, although controversially, that children who were given multi-vitamin supplements did perform better academically than children who were not.

The controversy centred around the question of diet. Did children not on supplements perform poorly because their diet lacked the necessary vitamins and minerals? Conversely, if a child eats a well-balanced diet does he or she need supplements? The jury still seems to be out on this one. What we can conclude, however, is that if you want to perform to your academic maximum it is vital to eat a diet that is well balanced and full of the necessary vitamins and minerals, especially when you are still growing.

DIET: THE JUNK PROBLEM

The problem is that most teenagers live on a diet that is extremely unbalanced. Usually it consists of food that has been processed in some way – junk food, fast food, food and drink that is heavy in salt, fat, sugars and artificial colourings and additives. Studies in America show some teenagers from affluent backgrounds are actually suffering from malnutrition because their diet is so poor. They are eating plenty – it's just that the food they are eating is completely lacking in balance and the required vitamins and minerals.

So What Should I Eat?
Eat a balanced diet though it's easier said than done. A diet of burgers, chips, bars, crisps and soft drinks is not a balanced diet though that is what many of us live on.

WHAT IS A BALANCED DIET?

It is a diet that has foods from all the main nutrition categories:

Protein
Essential to build bones and muscle and repair the body. Protein comes from meat, fish or pulses like beans and lentils. It is a good idea to vary your protein source and

alternate meat and vegetarian protein sources. Meat contains hidden fat so it is good to mix in beans and pulses.

Carbohydrates
Provide the energy essential for those preparing for exams. Potatoes are good sources of carbohydrates but these are often eaten in the form of chips which are full of fat. So it is a good idea to alternate your chips with carbohydrate-rich foods like pasta, brown bread or rice.

Fibre
Studies show that lack of fibre is one of the curses of our western diet. It can lead to poor digestion and ultimately to bowel cancer. Some young people have little or no fibre in their diets for the simple reason that it is entirely removed in the process of refinement that most foods go through nowadays. For example, proper brown flour has to have the best part, the husk, removed in order to make it white. It is essential to have a diet that is high in fibre. Start the day with a bowl of bran cereal – there are many good ones on the market. Try to eat wholegrain brown bread as well as white. Eat fresh fruit, vegetables and nuts. End the day with a bowl of bran cereal.

Fat
We all need fat in our diet. The problem lies in where we get our fat: mainly animal products such as meat, eggs, cheese, butter and cream. These are all saturated fats and their over-use is associated with heart disease. Heart disease is not exclusively associated with old age. Autopsies on young Americans killed in Vietnam, whose average age was nineteen, found alarming evidence of heart disease in many of the young victims. It is no coincidence that in Mediterranean countries, where the fat sources are mainly

non-animal products like olive oil, the incidence of heart disease is lower.

Try to cut back on your fat intake. Remember that many processed foods, such as biscuits, bars, cake, burgers, ice-cream, contain hidden fat. Try low-fat alternatives which are now readily available.

If you develop a weight problem, either too much weight (obesity) or too little weight (anorexia), seek professional help, initially from your GP.

Salt

We eat far too much salt. Watch your salt intake and remember salt is 'hidden' in many foods such as biscuits and cereals. You may not need to add any salt to your food.

VITAMIN AND MINERAL SUPPLEMENTS?

A well balanced diet rich in fresh fruit, vegetables and natural products such as fish, should give you enough vitamins and minerals. If you feel your diet is lacking in essential nutrients and for some reason you don't think you can easily improve it, a general vitamin and mineral supplement may help you to study. Talk to your local doctor or pharmacist and they will advise you on a suitable product.

CLEANING TOXINS FROM THE SYSTEM

The body and mind form an incredibly complex and highly sensitive system. The body reacts to the smallest changes in the environment. Just notice how you feel in a stuffy room after half an hour. You become weary and lethargic and your concentration diminishes. This is the body reacting to air and temperature changes.

What would happen to the delicate mechanism of a watch if you dropped fat, sugar and black oily tar (from cigarettes) on to it? Well that is what many of us do to our bodies! Then we get frustrated when the mechanism – our bodies – doesn't work well. Use the checklist below to see what may be clogging up your own system.

THINGS THAT POISON YOU OR BUNG YOU UP

POISONS – VERY HARMFUL

- Mood-altering drugs like cannabis, heroin, cocaine, ecstasy. These seriously mess up your body and your mind, making it almost impossible to function normally. Abuse of them can also lead to deadly infections like HIV and Hepatitis B.
- Cigarettes. These clog up the lungs and arteries, and may become a serious long-term addiction, causing life-threatening diseases.
- Alcohol. Excessive consumption of alcohol seriously impairs vision, judgement, concentration and general health. It also leads to long-term addiction and serious health and emotional problems.

THINGS THAT AFFECT THE SYSTEM

- *Excess sugar:* gives you an energy surge followed by a 'downer'. Avoid excess sugar in sweets and drinks. It alters your mood and will cause weight gain.
- *EMF* (electro-magnetic force). This comes from being too close to televisions or computer screens. New EC directives, for example, prohibit pregnant women from being exposed to VDU screens for too long. Studies show that young people watch on average four hours of television per day. This cannot be a good

thing. Television certainly disrupts study and being an essentially passive medium – you sit and absorb it – it can disrupt creative thought processes. It is therefore wise to limit your television viewing or video-game playing. Use them as treats or rewards when you have completed essential study.

- Junk food. With much convenience food and fast food, the natural goodness is lost. Filling yourself with junk food will result in a junk performance. Food is energy. Would you put methylated spirits in the tank of your car and expect it to go well? So fill your 'car' with good, fresh, natural foods.

TIPS

Every day try to take a breath of good, fresh natural air. Eat at least one bowl of bran cereal, a piece of fresh fruit and try to have fresh vegetables with your main meal. Finally, drink plenty of water. You can drink as much as you like. Whether it is tap or spring water is a matter of taste and money. But try to drink a minimum of eight glasses a day. It revives you and cleanses your system of toxins.

OTHER WORRIES

Sexual activity can expose you to the HIV virus which leads to AIDS. There are only two ways to protect your body from the virus. Abstinence – having no intimate sexual contact – is 100 per cent safe. The second is what is called 'safe' sex where a condom is used as a protection in intercourse. It must be noted that this method is not absolutely safe as condoms do have a failure rate, depending on how they are used.

If you have any doubts consult someone you can confide in, someone who will have your best interests at

Do I Fill Myself up with Gunge?

heart, such as a sympathetic parent, teacher, priest or GP. If you find it impossible to talk to any of these use a confidential helpline like the Samaritans who can provide you with professional help.

Remember everyone has difficulties and nothing is more stressful than worrying about your health or other personal problems like your love life. These can ruin your chances of doing well in exams so it is vital to talk to someone you can trust.

THE POWER SNOOZE – HOW RESTING GETS YOU BETTER RESULTS

Recent studies in America show that taking a nap or 'power snooze' during the day or early evening can be highly beneficial in several ways. It can give you quality rest which helps the immune system to recharge and fight infection. It gives the brain a chance to rest and switch off. Some studies suggest that a forty-minute cat-nap can be as effective as two to three hours of normal sleep. It may also allow the brain to go into the problem-solving mode, where the unconscious begins to digest conscious problems, giving a new perspective on them. The power snooze allows you to take a break from the pressure of exams.

HOW TO TAKE A POWER SNOOZE

Find a warm comfortable place where you will not be disturbed. Plump up some cushions, draw the curtains and slip off your shoes. Take the phone off the hook and play some relaxing music. Here is where you can use the *Maximum Points – Minimum Panic* audio tape, whose gentle music and lapping waves will lull you to sleep.

If you get used to cat-napping, your body will soon

come to look forward to its daily rest. You will even be able to train yourself to sleep and wake almost on command. I cat-nap or power-snooze daily, usually at around 6 pm when the day's work is over but before the night's activities have begun. I find it gives me a clear head and an amazing surge of energy. It is the perfect antidote to stress and exam burnout.

WORRY AND HOW TO DEAL WITH IT

Professor Eugene Gendlin of the University of Chicago made a profound discovery over twenty years ago. He was investigating why it was that certain people made strides in their therapy while many did not. He discovered that the successful clients held their problems in a particular physically felt way that inevitably led to a form of resolution.

This extraordinary process he called 'focusing'. Having discovered how successful clients solve their problems he went on to see if the process could be taught and after many years of research, found that it could. In fact he found it was a very natural process that young and old alike could learn.

I have had the privilege of training in the focusing method with Professor Gendlin in Chicago and I can apply some of the points of his research to the thorny question of exam worry in particular and life worries in general.

First we will do a simple exercise, focusing on our current worries. Remember that worry takes up a lot of our energy – either in suppressing it or in trying to solve the problem in our heads, where it often keeps going round and round with no definite solution.

HOW TO LET WORRY EXPRESS ITSELF

Sit quietly and let your attention settle on your stomach. Take a few breaths just to notice how you are and notice how your stomach feels. Then ask yourself this question; 'Is there anything in my life right now that is getting in the way of my happiness?'

Wait for the question to sink right into the core of your stomach, the centre of your body. At first you may find your head firing off answers quickly. 'Well of course there is,' it will say. 'There's this and that . . .' But that's not what we're looking for. You know that already. No, we're looking for something deeper, something half-felt; like a slight tightening in the stomach or chest. Often a picture will come with the feeling, like the image of a fist or the word 'tight'. And if you focus on the place in the stomach and give it some of your attention it may slowly become clearer until you sense that the tight feeling is actually to do with not having finished a project or a sense of regret at having been nasty to someone. If you keep giving it your attention, allowing it time to say why it is there, it will eventually tell you and you will feel an immediate physical relief.

It is a bit like leaving the house and half-way into town getting a tiny queasy feeling that you have forgotten something. It is your body that senses this, not your conscious mind. The mind will take several moments to locate exactly what you forgot. 'Was it putting out the cat?' No. 'Turning off the lights?' No. 'Bringing all my books?' No. All this time the body is still feeling uneasy; it already knows you have forgotten something and is waiting for the conscious mind to catch up with it and find out what.

Finally the mind comes up trumps: 'I forgot to leave the key with the neighbour for Jane and she won't be able to get in.' That's it! Now notice what happens to the vague tight feeling in the body when the mind finally remembers. The tightening disappears. It is exactly the same with focusing on stress. Your body knows that something is wrong and feels uneasy. Usually we do everything we can to get rid of that vague uneasy feeling. We'll deny it, suppress it, ignore it, work through it, try to obliterate it or numb it with alcohol or drugs. Yet all the time it is actually the gateway to a solution to one of your problems. It is actually the wisdom of the whole body trying to knock on the door of the conscious mind to tell it something is wrong. If you really try to listen to your feelings in this way you will soon find that you will tap into the vast wisdom of your body's innate, intuitive intelligence. And then watch what happens!

Research in focusing now shows that this approach can be applied to literally every situation in life, from focusing on a business decision to focusing on how to finish the final phase of a college project. It seems that this innate wisdom in us all can guide us in every area of our lives. There are details on focusing literature at the back of this book.

LOVE YOURSELF

Love is a confusing word. It's mixed up with so many things nowadays. You are even supposed to love Coca Cola and the brand of jeans you wear. But the love I am talking about here is more like the love that kept the rabbits alive in the animal experiment. Remember that? It was the quality attention of the lab attendant that that kept them alive longer than the rabbits that were simply fed and watered.

If we don't get attention we too will eventually shrivel up and die. Attention is love. You can tell your aged granny all you like that you love her but if you never take the time to get on the bus to spend an hour with her will she really believe she's loved? Love is attention and attention takes effort and time.

Give attention and time to looking after yourself by doing some of the things outlined in this chapter. Take time out for yourself to relax, walk, eat, sleep and play. One of the oldest spiritual commandments is: 'Love your neighbour as yourself'. The problem is that many of us do not love *ourselves* in a kind and respectful way. Is it really loving yourself to fill your lungs with tar or to push your body beyond its limits and into exhaustion and burnout?

This chapter has been all about looking after yourself. The pressures of becoming adult and passing exams are awesome and many individuals are overcome by them. The result is that many entering adult life and the workforce are already stressed out, addictive people. Is it any wonder that so many relationships break down under the pressure? If you put some of the above advice into practice you will be bringing quality attention to yourself. You will be loving or minding yourself in the fullest sense of the word. You can then go on to love and look after others.

Go on; do yourself a favour: *love yourself!*

6

HOW TO PASS EXAMS – A PERSONAL GUIDE

HOW THE BRAIN WORKS

Did you know that the brain is one of the wonders of the universe? Go on, put your hands up to your head and hold it! What you are holding contains about ten thousand million neurons! Can you imagine that, alive right now inside your head. Did you know that those neurons can make 10 to the power of 800 possible connections. That's ten multiplied by itself 800 times, almost an infinite number.

Just reading this page requires an almost limitless number of brain cell connections. Did you know that right now in your head between 10,000 and a million chemicals are at work, transferring thoughts, making cell connections, retaining memory, synthesising material, coordinating sight, smell, sound, taste, breathing, heartbeat, memory, feeling – the very substance of consciousness.

It's estimated we may use only 2 per cent of our brain's capacity. We don't even know just what our brains are capable of. You carry the miracle of the universe on your shoulders right now and you can probably do anything you put your magnificent mind to.

It's our job now to give it the chance to work for you, an exciting prospect.

RIGHT VERSUS LEFT BRAIN

Your brain is divided into two hemispheres, the right and the left.

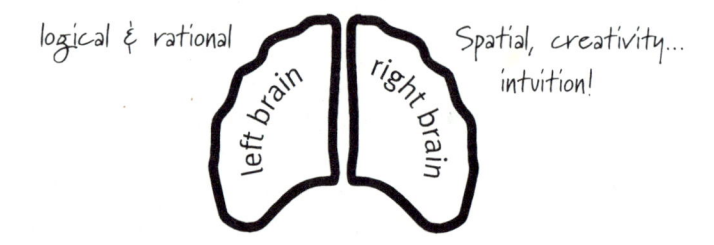

logical & rational — left brain | right brain — *Spatial, creativity... intuition!*

Traditionally western man has tended to favour the left hemisphere. There are several historical reasons for this, including the fact that speech, print and writing are all linear in form. They run in sequence from left to right. Because of this it was assumed that the whole of the brain was linear and logical and that everything came in neat lists.

The educational system teaches everyone in roughly the same way, even though it is now known that some people have more developed 'right' brains and would learn better if taught in a different, right-brain way. Recent research shows that the right brain is just as important as the left. It deals with space, colour, light, music and creativity. It is intuitive rather than logical, spontaneous rather than rational, and approaches learning and life in a more open, instinctive way than the more logical left brain.

We know that we can learn from the overall shape, colour, look and feel of a thing as well as its logical sequence and structure. In fact it may be that the true synthesis of reality lies literally at the 'centre' of the brain, perhaps in the limbic system, possibly the hypothalamus, where right and left hemispheres, the thinking and feeling, the logical and intuitive, all come together in a glorious, transcendent whole.

HOW DOES THIS KNOWLEDGE AFFECT MY STUDY?

In several key ways: firstly in the way we take notes – the very basis of our study.

NOTE-TAKING

The traditional way to take notes is in written form, sentence after sentence, until you have a small book of notes on the subject. This goes back to the very discovery of writing. (Only now with the advent of computer-learning technology are we finding different, more graphic ways, of presenting material.)

IS THIS EFFECTIVE?

No, not really. For one thing, it's a nightmare to revise such long notes. Also the brain remembers and interprets pictures, maps and graphs much better than pages of closely written sentences. Let us look at a simple example. Below are the two basic ways of getting across information – the traditional notes and the newer form of 'note-maps'. Decide for yourself which is easier to understand and easier to recall and memorise. The subject for this exercise is the profit and expenses profile of a restaurant.

TRADITIONAL NOTE-TAKING

Operating costs and profit of the La Traviata Pizza Company restaurant for the year ending 1995 were as follows: Purchase of food accounted for 22.4 per cent of income. Wages accounted for 18.2 per cent of income. Advertising accounted for 19.8 per cent of income and that left a profit of 39.6 per cent of all monies taken in.

NOTE-MAPPING FORM

La Traviata Pizza Company
Profit and costs

Question
Which is easier to take in, understand and remember?
Answer
The second is easier because it is graphic and represents the information, namely the costs and profits of the company, in terms of graphics and the division of space.

If you added colour and attractive design features, like a cartoon character representing 'a big fat profit' you would understand and remember the information even better.

HOW CAN I MAP OUT MY NOTES?

Let us look at a typical class. We will take, for example, a one-hour geography lecture on 'The Disappearing Rain Forests of Brazil'. If you are not used to mapping, begin by taking traditional notes.

TRADITIONAL CLASS NOTES ON THE DISAPPEARING RAIN FORESTS OF BRAZIL

Amount of rain forest disappearing: an area approximately the size of Wales disappears every year.

Tribal population dying: from imported diseases, violent settlers and the hazards of fleeing the encroaching development.

Effect on local flora: plants unique to the rain forest that provide vital medicine and drugs are being permanently lost with incalculable effects for medical research.

Effect on local fauna: animals and insects unique to this area of the world becoming extinct with permanent loss to world's genetic pool.

Global impact of 'greenhouse effect': loss of rain forest adds to global warming. Vast fires raging year round as forest burns.

Lack of action by Brazilian government: they will not take action until the West cleans up its own pollution.

Future: loss of rain forests equivalent of losing a vital lung that helps clean up the world atmosphere and regulate CO_2 pollution and global warming.

Now let's look at a summary of all that information in map form.

Brazilian Rainforest
lecture

Brazilian Rainforest lecture

- **Brazilian government inaction**
  blames West for own pollution

- **Area loss**
  - size of Wales - each year

- **Flora loss**
  loss to medicine cures research

- **Fauna loss**
  to animal gene pool

- **Tribal loss**
  permanent loss of native life due to disease and violence

- **Global Lung**
  keeps down CO_2, Global warming — now in jeprody

- **Long term**
  damage to the world's climate, environment and genetic pool

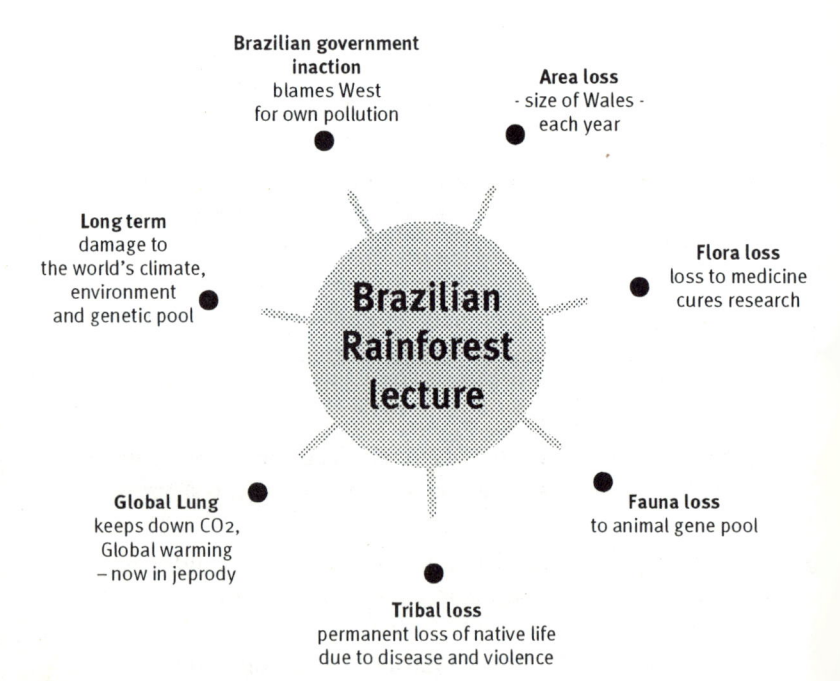

TIPS ON MAPPING

- *Keep it coloured.* Use colours for headings and highlighting.
- *Keep it simple.* One-word headings will help the mind to recall the rest of the information.

NOW I HAVE EFFECTIVE MAP-NOTES HOW DO I REMEMBER THEM?

Question

If you attend a class and don't think about the content again for twenty-four hours, how much of it will you forget in a day?

Tick

- ☐ None
- ☐ 10 per cent
- ☐ 40 per cent
- ☐ 80 per cent
- ☐ All of it

Answer

I will forget 80 per cent.

Unbelievable but true. Attend a class and within a day you will remember only 20 per cent. And that is not going to help you to pass exams.

HOW MUCH I REMEMBER OF MY CLASS

In the thirty minutes after a class ends you remember more about the class than you were taught. Why? It's because the information in the class triggers off all sorts of associations with the knowledge you already have. That is why it is vital to revise and put long notes into simple 'map' revision form as soon after the class as possible. If you do, just look what happens to your memory.

What happens to your memory
within 24 hours of a lecture

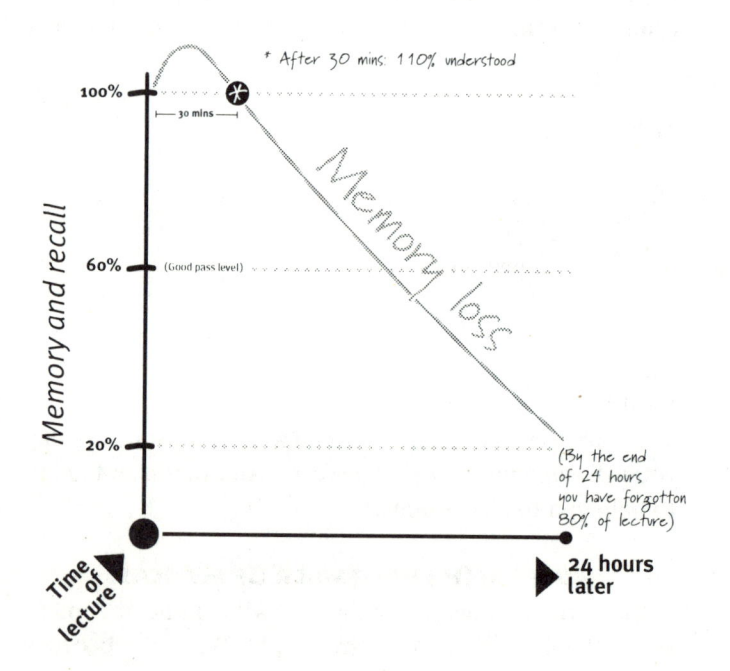

† After 30 mins: 110% understood

100% — ✳
|— 30 mins —|

Memory loss

60% — (Good pass level)

Memory and recall

20% — (By the end of 24 hours you have forgotten 80% of lecture)

Time of lecture ▶   ▶ 24 hours later

Revision within 30 minutes of classes
leads to high recall level

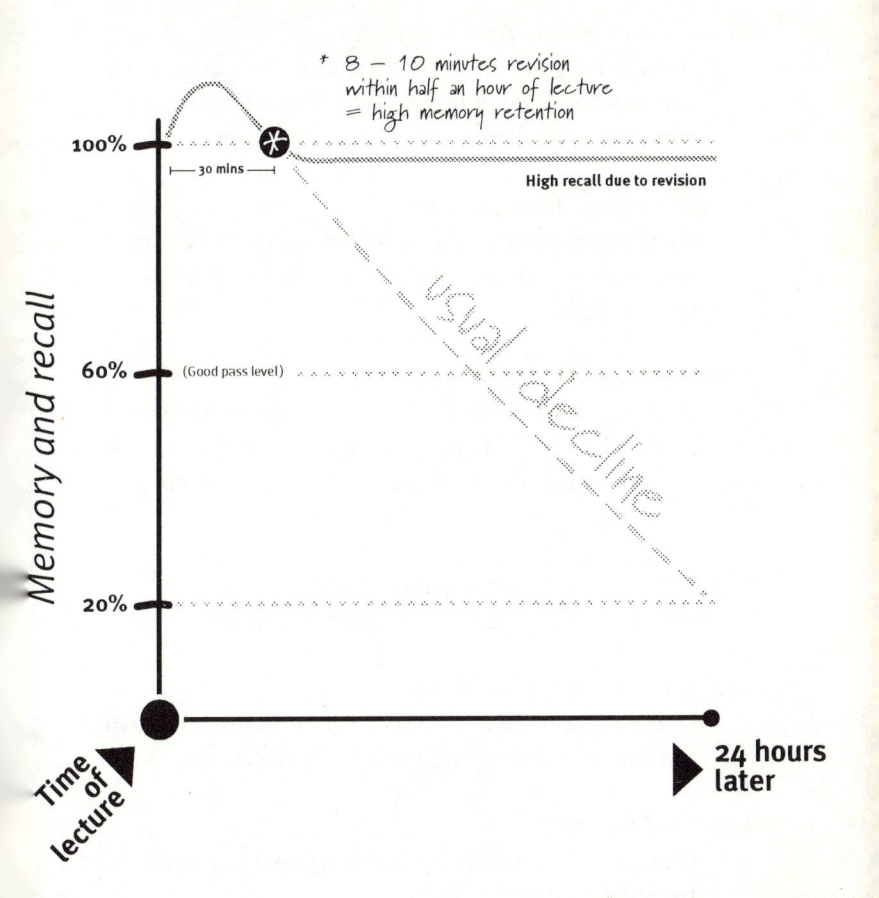

8 – 10 minutes revision within half an hour of lecture = high memory retention

Memory and recall

- 100%
- 30 mins
- High recall due to revision
- 60% (Good pass level)
- Usual decline
- 20%

Time of lecture → 24 hours later

You have to spend only an initial eight to ten minutes revising and putting your notes into map form. Do you need to revise more after that? Yes.

THE SIX-STEP REVISION PLAN

First revision, twenty-four hours later
> Draw out or imagine note-map again. Only then check it against original note-map. Check just how accurate you were after four to six minutes' revision.

Second revision, one week later
> Draw out or imagine the same note-map again. Check after four to six minutes' revision to see how much you got right.

Third revision, one month later
> Sit down and try to draw the rain forest note-map again. Then check it against original. Check after two to four minutes' revision to see how much you remember.

Fourth revision: in your revision period
> Draw out map and check it against original.

Fifth revision, before mock exams
> Draw out map and check it against original. Do two to four minutes' revision and see how you do.

Sixth and final revision:
> Draw out map and then check it against original (two to four minutes' revision).

The 6 step revision approach
keeps your memory up in the high zone

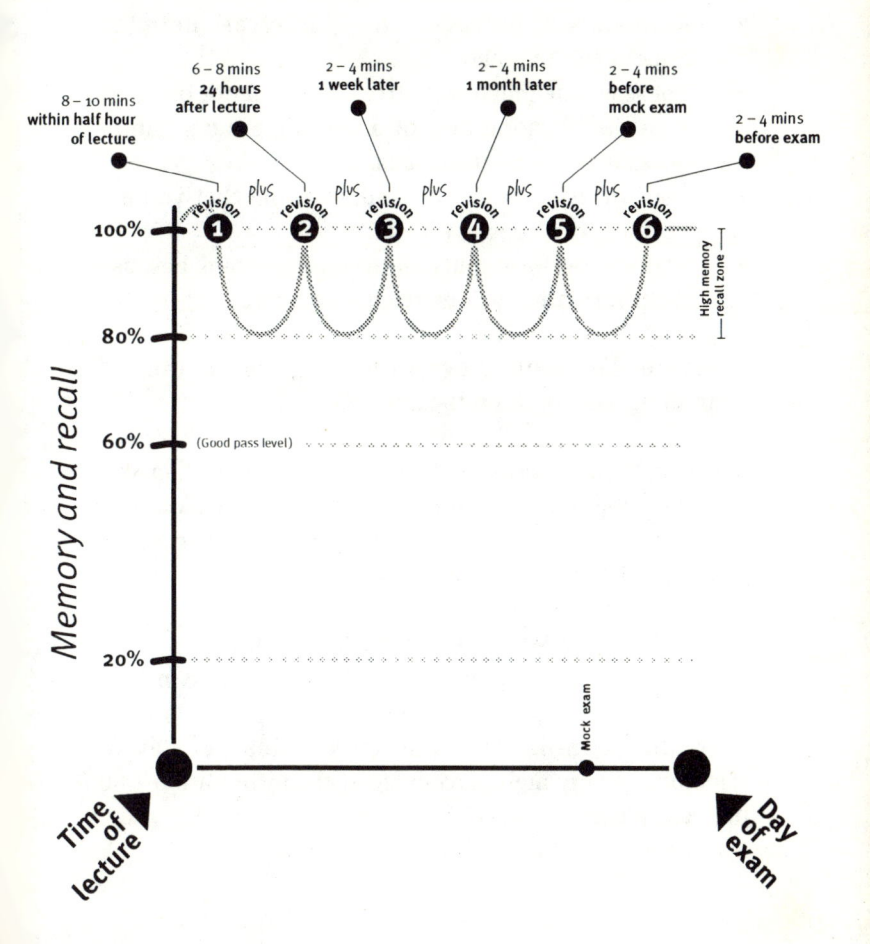

- **8 – 10 mins** within half hour of lecture — revision 1
- **6 – 8 mins** 24 hours after lecture — revision 2
- **2 – 4 mins** 1 week later — revision 3
- **2 – 4 mins** 1 month later — revision 4
- **2 – 4 mins** before mock exam — revision 5
- **2 – 4 mins** before exam — revision 6

Memory and recall

- 100%
- 80% — High memory recall zone
- 60% (Good pass level)
- 20%

Time of lecture → Mock exam → Day of exam

ADVANTAGES OF SIX-STEP REVISION

- You will remember more of the material as you are not giving your mind the chance to forget it. (Most revision is a nightmare because students are really learning all over again. They have allowed the mind to forget the material.)
- Revision will be easier and quicker as the mind remembers the map.
- There will be much less stress. You will not be faced with the daunting task of a revising a mountain of notes just before the exams.
- You will have peace of mind, knowing that you are keeping up to date with your work
- You will perform much better in the exams because the information will be readily available.

Compare the graph above with the graph of the old 'cramming' approach on the next page.

If you note-map and use the Six-Step Revision Plan you will remember 80 per cent or more of the information by the time of the exam – more than is required for a very good mark!

HOW MUCH TIME WILL IT TAKE?

If the class were in September and the exams were in June it would cost you only thirty minutes of revision spread over nine months. That's seven seconds per day to remember a very high percentage of the information – 80 per cent plus.

DISADVANTAGES OF CRAMMING

CRAMMING IS VERY INEFFECTIVE

After twenty to forty minutes' of study time your retention and comprehension levels plummet until after two to three hours you will remember little or nothing. Cramming by definition involves long stints of intense study, so forget it – it just doesn't work.

CRAMMING IS VERY STRESSFUL

Your unconscious knows that you have forgotten most of the material and it is dreading having to cram all that material into a few short hours just before exams. This thought alone produces extreme stress.

CRAMMING IS EXHAUSTING

The process of cramming leads to mental and physical exhaustion.

CRAMMING WON'T HELP YOU TO PASS YOUR EXAMS

The inefficiency, stress and exhaustion of cramming will mean that you are less likely to get decent grades – so all that stress and effort is wasted.

HOW CAN I MAKE MY HOMEWORK EASIER AND MORE EFFECTIVE?

Never study a subject for more than thirty to forty minutes. Keep in mind the chart on the next page.

After forty minutes take a break for five to ten minutes before going back to study.

Old "cramming" approach
... leads to poor memory
and possibility of poor marks & failure

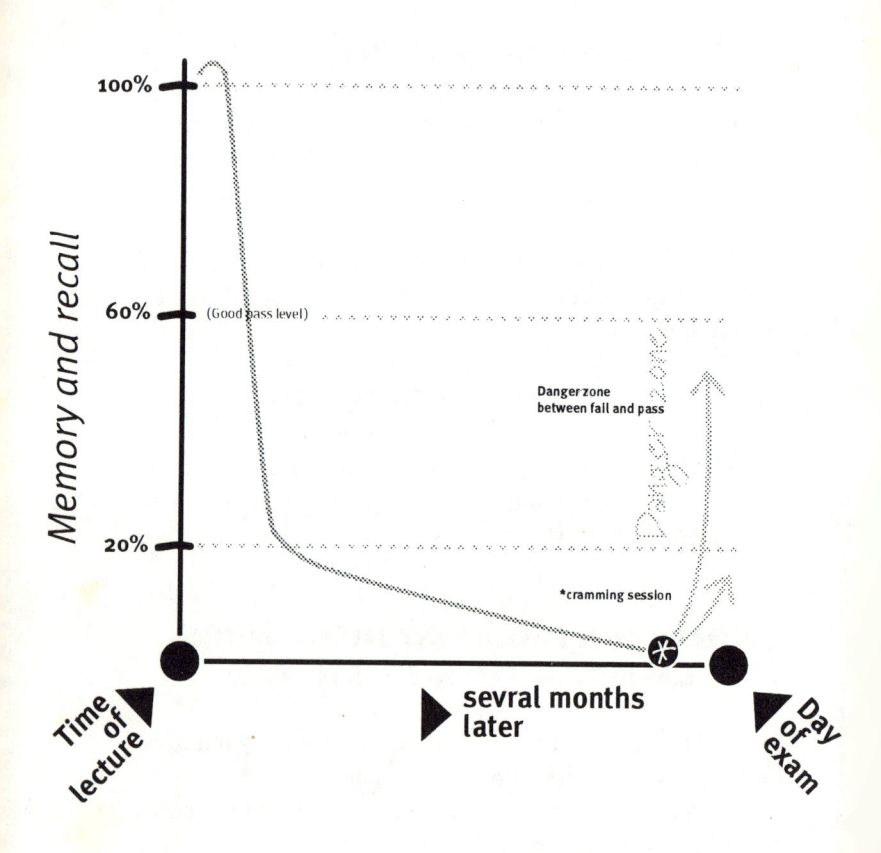

- 100%
- 60% (Good pass level)
- 20%

Memory and recall

Danger zone between fail and pass

*cramming session

Time of lecture ▶ sevral months later ▶ Day of exam

What Should I Do in the Break?
Research shows that it doesn't matter what you do so long as you don't study.

Do
- Get up from your desk, stretch and move around.
- Take a breath of fresh air; it helps to clear the head.
- Have a cup of tea, drink and chat. Social contact is healthy and breaks isolation.

Don't
- Watch television. If you get interested in a programme you may not have the willpower to go back to study after ten minutes.
- Phone a friend. You may get stuck in a long conversation with similar results. Keep the phone call as a treat for when you have finished your night's homework.
- Smoke or drink coffee or alcohol. These will give you an artificial high that will be followed by a low. Then you get into the addictive cycle and will have to have another high just to pick you up again.

EFFECTIVE HOMEWORK OR STUDY SESSION

TIP

If you can limit your work to three subjects it will bring homework down to three hours, which is quite enough material to remember and digest. However coming up to exams the pressure increases and you may need to study four subjects. If you have been revising regularly and note-

What happens when you study for over 40 minutes

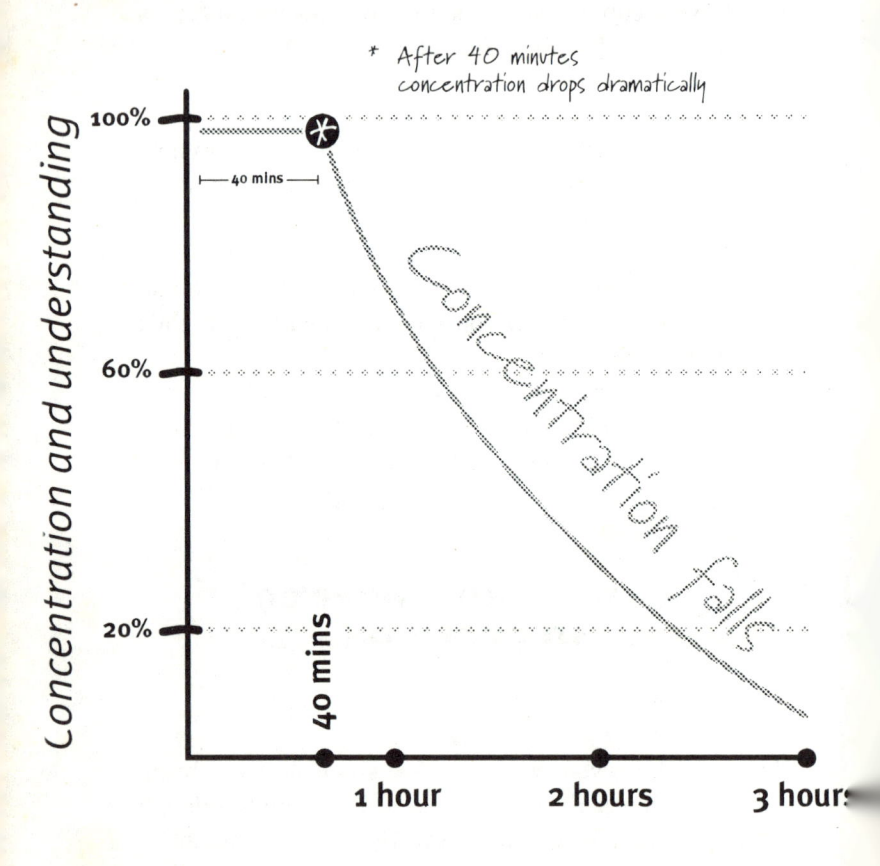

Concentration and understanding (y-axis): 100%, 60%, 20%

x-axis: 40 mins, 1 hour, 2 hours, 3 hours

* After 40 minutes concentration drops dramatically

Concentration falls

mapping you will notice a huge difference in your retention and will end up, over a six-month period, needing to study less, not more.

IMPORTANT

- Never drop the breaks or revision periods. You may think you're working harder but you're only working less efficiently and you will have to do more work in the end just to catch up.

REMEMBER IF IT IS EXAMS YOU WANT TO PASS

- Map your notes.
- Use the Six-Step Revision Plan.
- Study only for forty minutes at a time with a ten-minute break.
- Don't cram.
- Never study for more than four hours at a time even with breaks.

If you do all the above you will remember and understand 80 per cent plus of your required material. With that level of knowledge it would be difficult to fail any exam. In fact you will probably do very well.

OTHER TIPS TO MAKE STUDY PLEASANT

- Make your study area comfortable. As you are going to spend a lot of your time studying it is important to be comfortable there.
- Put a 'Do Not Disturb' sign on the door or tell people you are not to be disturbed. Have someone take phone messages and break your study only if it is urgent.
- If you set rules stick to them. Then people will know

How to put together an effective homework or study session

study 40 mins   *break* 10 mins   *revise* 5 mins

- subject 1 — 40 mins
- break 10 mins
- revise sub1 — 5 mins
- subject 2 — 40 mins
- break 10 mins
- revise sub2 — 5 mins
- subject 3 — 40 mins
- break 10 mins
- revise sub3 — 5 mins
- subject 4 — 40 mins
- break 10 mins
- revise sub4 — 5 mins
- revise past course material — 25 mins

4 hours total

not to phone you during your 7 pm-10 pm study period. Remember it is difficult enough to study; it is doubly difficult to resume study once you've been unnecessarily disturbed and distracted.
- Have a clear desk. Clutter distracts. Put your desk in order and notice the difference in your concentration.
- Have everything you need at hand. It is impossible to study if you suddenly find that you have left a vital book at school or you don't have a compass or a calculator. Draw up a list of what you need to bring home from school every day.
- Use a comfortable chair. Posture is very important in study. If you are uncomfortable or your back is not supported you can't study comfortably. Get a chair that is right for you. It should have correct height, good back support and a comfortable cushion.
- Make sure the lighting is adequate. Studying in poor light leads to headaches, poor concentration and sloppy work. Try to have two sources of lighting: good background light e.g. from a strong white overhead bulb and direct lighting from a desk light, preferably one you can move about.
- Have proper heating and ventilation. Studies show that our environment is vital for good performance. You will study better in a room that is warm but well ventilated. Make sure you have a window ajar or some source of fresh air, otherwise drowsiness will interfere with your concentration.

STUDY DISTRACTIONS – THE 'HIT LIST'

The best laid study plans and the nicest studying den can all be blown apart by – the distraction. The problem with distractions is that we often bring them in to our study camp ourselves, like traitors or spies, and then allow them to blow up our study strategies. The main distractions are:

- Phone calls which can creep in at any time and often look innocent: 'He only wants a quick word,' is the message that comes up the stairs. Resist it. A quick word can become twenty minutes and your whole study schedule is blown apart. Phoning back can be a reward for work done; you can then talk for as long as you like. People will soon get the message that you don't take calls while studying and they'll phone outside study time. They will also develop a respect for your willpower.
- Drop-in friends are an even worse danger because a short chat can develop into an hour-long game of *Ridge Racer* on the Playstation or a minute-by-minute account of your Saturday night date – which with proper prompting and discussion could take all night. Remedy as for phone calls. Delegate someone to tell your friend you'll call around later as right now you're studying. Then you will have something to look forward to when you've finished.
- Television. Did you ever notice how magnetic television sets are? It's as if they have a special power. You intend to ignore the set but something stops you. And something else strange happens when you are about to study: television programmes that would otherwise not be given a second look, say if you were going out to a movie or to see friends, suddenly become fascinating. You just have to sit down and watch them. You say silly things like: 'I'll only watch for a minute', 'I'll only watch it until the ads' and then you go on to sit right through until the *News at Ten*.

ARE YOU BEING HIT BY DISTRACTIONS?
T.V.
PHONE CALLS
LATEST PULP C.D.
COMPUTER GAMES
POW!
CUP OF TEA
BAM!
HOME & AWAY
FRIENDS
STUDY SHELTER

By that time you've really blown your study period. Remedy: don't go near the set. It's far too dangerous. Get family members to promise either to switch it off when you sit down during study-time (except for *Coronation Street* of course) or to eject you from the room. I'm sorry but it is the only solution.

- Cups of tea or coffee, drinks of Coke, cigarettes. Since you have a ten-minute break every forty minutes, you can have three or four cuppas over an evening. But bring your alarm clock with you or get someone in the family to push you up the stairs after ten minutes; otherwise you're doomed.
- Reading newspapers/books/magazines. Ever noticed how really boring books on gardening or DIY or eighteen-month-old copies of *Woman's Own* can suddenly become fascinating while you're supposed to be studying. As with viewing, forty minutes can disappear while you read about 'grouting the outside toilet' or 'how 1989 will be a great year for Leo lovers' and you are not even a Leo! There is only one remedy. Pick the magazines up, pile them outside your room and see just how attractive they are at 11.30 pm when you've finally finished your study. I promise you won't even glance at them.
- Making phone calls is even worse than taking them. This time you are paying (or more than likely someone else is) to be distracted when you know you should be studying so your conscience annoys you as well. Remedy: get a member of the family to come down and politely but firmly say within earshot: 'I'm sorry but I need the phone right now. My Tai Chi teacher is calling long distance from Beijing and I can't afford to miss him.' That gives you an excuse to end the conversation.

- Wandering mind. As we saw earlier the mind has one thousand million cells and it's strange how they all start humming with distracting ideas every time you sit down to study seventeenth-century law reform. Suddenly anything is more interesting and the head just fills with images, pictures, ideas, in fact anything but the subject in hand. Another strange thing happens – the more you try to study the more your mind wanders. Remedy: acknowledge the distraction! Let it know you know it's there; then find a suitable place next to you like a soft cushion on the bed and place it there telling it you will come back to it as soon as you have finished. You will be amazed just how well this works. Worries are really like toddlers; they cry until they get attention. Once they are acknowledged they go back to their own little games. It is ignoring them and telling them to go away that drives them mad. It's the same with your wandering worries, just acknowledge and stack them next to you and tell them you'll be back. By the time you've finished your study they'll usually be gone.
- CDs, video games – in fact anything that happens to come to hand. Did you ever notice how the most bizarre things can begin to attract you while you are studying or, more dangerously, about to study. Sometimes it can be really interesting things like a new computer game or the latest Cranberries CD. More often it can be something completely weird, something you'd never give a thought to if you were getting ready to go on a date or hit the town, something that becomes attractive only because you are trying to study. Like sitting with your ears cocked trying to decipher what your neighbours are saying through the bedroom wall, or tuning aimlessly into foreign

radio stations or watching a toddler next door play for hours in his sand pit.

DISTRACTIONS – THE REAL TRUTH

And now can be revealed for the first time the real truth behind distractions. We actually allow ourselves to be distracted. Why? There are several reasons – find which one fits you. This knowledge may be the key to setting yourself free from them

- All this study is too much effort. At heart I may not be up to giving it all this time. I may be a bit lazy.
- I may go to all this trouble just to fail. At bottom I may not believe I can succeed.
- I'll never get good enough grades, no matter how hard I study.
- I can't be bothered. My real talents may lie in another career like being a rock star.

There are countless other reasons for distractions. Take a moment to reflect and find out exactly what is at the bottom of your distraction and lack of concentration. It will repay your time: knowing the cause puts you in the way of finding a solution.

If you are regularly distracted, no matter how hard you try not to be, then it's time to reflect on what's really going on. If you can't find the solution talk to someone you can trust who may be able to help you see what it is.

STUDY TIPS – HOW TO BE MORE EFFECTIVE IN LESS TIME

DEAD TIME

Some people have really weird jobs – much weirder than working Saturdays in the supermarket. Did you know, for example, that someone (probably a behavioural scientist) once calculated how much time the average person spends queuing in a lifetime. (Queuing is defined as waiting in line, waiting for – people to arrive, meetings to start, programmes to come on, buses to turn up, lifts to come, lights to turn green, etc . . .) Go on, guess the answer . . .

I'll even give you a choice:
one week?
one month?
six months?
one year?
eighteen months?

The answer is – eighteen months!

Now stop a moment and let that sink in. That's a full seventy-eight weeks or 546 days or 13,104 hours, or over three quarters of a million seconds.

Look at your watch for one minute and just sit there waiting until the minute is up. It seems like a long time. That's what we human beings spend a lot of our time doing – just waiting. It's mind-boggling really. What could you do in eighteen uninterrupted months? You could write a bestseller, learn to speak a language fluently, acquire a whole new skill like playing a musical instrument. What do you do instead? You just wait there.

I call this waiting time 'dead time' and I just may have a use for it. First let's identify your dead time, time when you are waiting or travelling or queuing or in-between things. Put a tick if you spend more than five minutes daily doing any one of these things:

- ☐ travelling to school or college
- ☐ walking to the shops
- ☐ walking to a friend's house
- ☐ waiting for lifts
- ☐ waiting for meals to be ready
- ☐ waiting to fall asleep
- ☐ waiting for a television show to come on
- ☐ waiting to get up
- ☐ waiting for something else [fill in]

Now add up all your dead time in a average day.

HOW TO USE DEAD TIME TO STUDY

Remember the mind-map of the Brazilian rain forest that we invited you to study earlier? Try replicating it on a piece of paper right now. If you can, then give yourself a slap on the back. If you can't you'll have to go back to p. 64 and study it for three to four minutes before we can go on.

OK? Now I want you to imagine you have forty-five minutes of dead time. You're standing at a bus stop, for example, daydreaming about Man United's coming second in the league again. Well, instead of that, spend the next five minutes recreating the mind-map of the Brazilian rain forest in your mind. Whatever you do don't look at the map until after that five minutes. Let your imagination go wild. Use colours, highlights, flashing lights, cartoon characters – in fact anything that will make the mental picture interesting and memorable. For example, use *imagery*. You can conjure up a picture of the rain forest dying slowly – it's sad but true and something you won't easily forget. All this will appeal to different aspects of your mind, the humorous part, the part that expresses anger, sympathy, feelings, the part that remembers figures and shape. The more parts of the brain you can appeal to and engage, the better chance you have of recreating the particular map.

And remember, you can do maps of anything – even sequential, logical, mathematical topics that usually have to be learnt laboriously in their exact sequence – you can make a 'map' story of them. Something that sums the whole thing up in a picture or image.

You can learn from your *feelings* also. Remember how you felt discovering those facts about the rain forest, the fact that we are killing off part of the planet. Feelings are important. The problem with left brain learning is that it is mainly logical and factual and devoid of feeling. But that does not represent how humans react to life. A lot of the subjects you study can quite easily engage your feelings.

USING FEELING IN LEARNING

Invite yourself to notice how you feel about the fact that the rain forest is fast disappearing. How does it feel knowing we as a race are destroying irreplaceable plants that some day could help medicine to cure terrible diseases? How do you feel knowing that the air you breathe will be hotter and dirtier as a result of this destruction?

If you can bring this feeling part into your learning you will open up a whole new and vibrant area of memory which will come to your aid when you try to remember things in exams. In fact do anything you can, anything that feels right, to remember the things that you study.

NOTE-MAP EXERCISE

1   Spend that five minutes of dead time trying to create the mind-map of the disappearing rain forest in your

head. Try to fill in the main headings and sub-headings.
2. After five minutes look up the map on p. 64 and see what you got right and what you missed out.
3. Close the book and spend a moment recreating the map in your head again before moving on to the next thing.

Did you find that whole exercise any easier than you would have found revising up to this? If you used all the parts of your brain, including your capacity for visualising and feeling when drawing the mind-map, you probably found it much easier than before.

What I am describing here is using holistic revision technique in your 'dead' time. Holistic revision is whole or full revision in which we use both sides of the brain to learn and understand through feelings and space as well as logic. Now, whenever you have a few minutes of otherwise dead time try using this holistic revision technique and you'll be amazed at what happens. Students I know have cut their study time in half simply by studying and revising in their dead time. The advantages are as follows:

- You will very efficiently learn your material. If you use the Six-Step Revision Plan covered earlier you will almost certainly remember 80 per cent plus of the material by the time of the exam.
- Revision and note-mapping in the head is the most appropriate way of preparing for real exams. Remember that you are allowed to take only your head into the examination and not your books. It makes very good sense therefore to do as much mental preparation as possible. This approach perfectly prepares you for the particular demands of our examination system. Use it and you will succeed.

USE YOUR FRIENDS TO HELP YOU TO PASS EXAMS

Have you ever noticed how much easier it is to go running or exercising with a friend? If the friend wasn't there you'd find some excuse not to go out. You feel much better going to a job interview with a friend. It's as if sharing the experience halves the pain and worry about it. Studies have repeatedly shown that most humans are sociable. Most of us need people because they:

- help us see ourselves more fully
- help us create and do things
- make us react to things they say and do
- share humour
- share feelings

It is difficult to laugh on your own. It is very difficult to share love and affection on your own. Ever tried kissing yourself? It's not as much fun as kissing someone else. The truth is that company can *stimulate* and *motivate* us. It's also an interesting fact that two of the things most missing in study are stimulation and motivation. Studying with a friend will help to:

- increase your motivation to study
- stimulate your interaction with the subject
- make you see how much you really understand your subject

This is a vital point. It is almost impossible to judge how well you know a subject yourself. It is very difficult to examine yourself, ask questions and answer them as well but a friend can do all this and help you see what you *actually* know.

HOW CAN I GET A FRIEND TO HELP ME TO STUDY?

Pick a time. It can be five minutes or fifty minutes. Use dead time. Let's look at the rain forest map again, this time seeing how you can use a friend to help you revise in 'dead time'. You are on the bus going home and you have a spare ten minutes so . . .

(i) Decide on a time, for example five minutes, for you to outline the rain forest map to your friend.
(ii) Describe the map of the rain forest including:
    (a) overall shape and subject
    (b) main headings
    (c) the key words

Your friend can look at the original map and:
(a) prompt you as you go along with yes or no answers
(b) encourage you when you have almost the right answer
(c) fill in the gaps when you have finished and give you an overall performance comment such as 'good', 'poor' or 'great'

Then switch around and do the same for your friend, guiding and assessing him while he describes a map of his choice. This helps you to see objectively exactly how much you know. It is also an excellent practice for exams because it's how you will be marked. Guiding and assessing your friend puts you in the mindset of the examiner. Now it is you who have to formulate questions, analyse answers and assess performance. It also gives you a more comprehensive grasp of your subject. Assessing someone else's knowledge really makes you think deeply and differently about the subject matter itself.

SHARED REVISION

This ten-minute exchange will give you a comprehensive, holistic view of your material and provide the means of approaching, assessing and examining it. I cannot recommend this shared revision too highly. It also encourages companionship and humour and can even make studying fun.

WHERE CAN I SHARE STUDY/REVISION TIME?

Anywhere, just find one other person. You can do it:

- while waiting for class
- before study
- during breaks
- after study to revise
- at lunch
- on the phone
- after school or college
- in fact anywhere, at any time. It's always an effective way of studying.

STRESS AND STUDY – A LETHAL COMBINATION

Do we need stress in our lives? Yes – some stress. Without demands and challenges in life we wouldn't get out of bed in the morning. Too much stress, however, and we tend towards burnout and end up back in bed – this time sick. So we need just enough stress to get us out of bed but not enough stress to put us back into it. It is vital to keep a balance and that is why it is so important to:

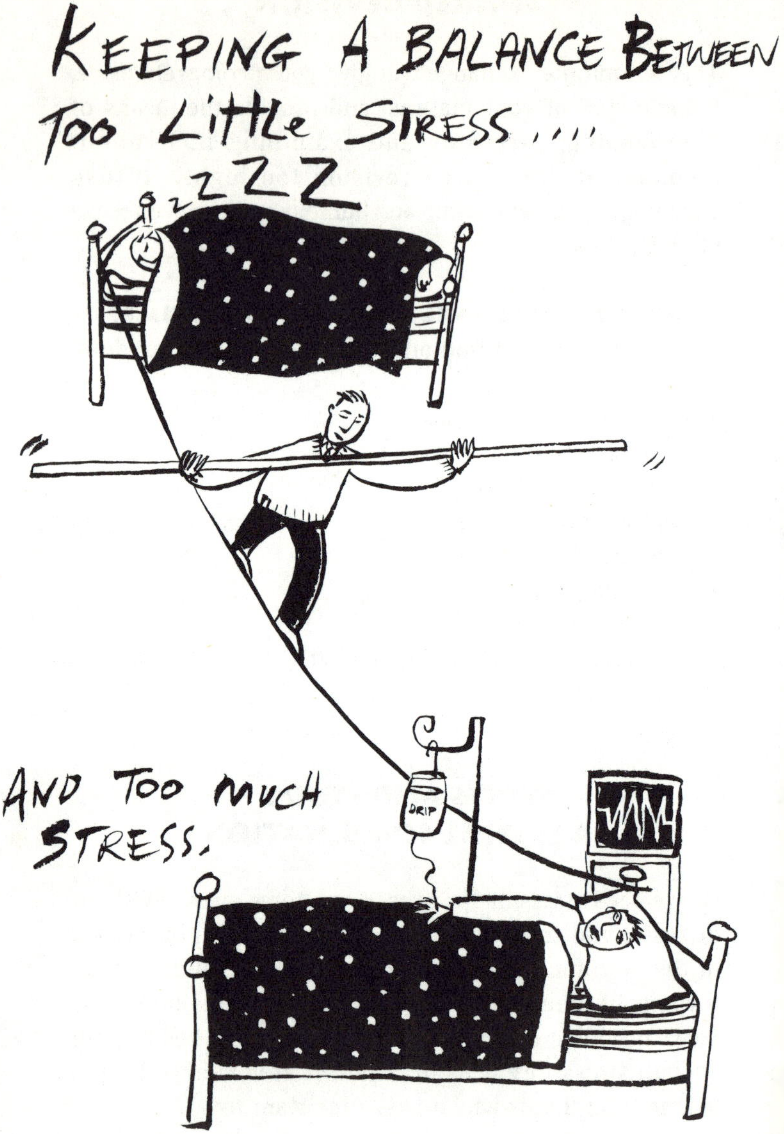
KEEPING A BALANCE BETWEEN
TOO LITTLE STRESS ....
zzZZ
DRIP
AND TOO MUCH
STRESS.

- sleep well
- exercise regularly
- eat well
- relax regularly
- study effectively

SOME FASCINATING FACTS

We have looked at how we can study effectively but before we leave this section I want to remind you of some fascinating facts:

- Within five minutes you will have forgotten up to 40 per cent of the class you've just attended.
- Within twenty-four hours you will have forgotten up to 80 per cent of the class.
- After thirty to forty minutes of study your ability to learn and remember drops dramatically.
- We remember approximately:
    20 per cent of what we read
    30 per cent of what we hear
    40 per cent of what we see
    50 per cent of what we say
    60 per cent of what we do
  but 90 per cent of what we read, hear, see, say and do.

So to make your learning fully effective and easy to remember always combine:

(i) reading the text *with*
(ii) having it read out *with*
(iii) seeing it in a mind-map form *with*
(iv) saying it out loud yourself *with*
(v) acting it out

- There are two main types of learning: *surface* learning and *deep* learning.

SURFACE LEARNING/DEEP LEARNING

This is when you learn things parrotlike, with the intention of repeating the same information in the exams.

Unfortunately the exam culture with its constant stream of assessments and tests encourages this form of quick learning. This means that students:

- do not really understand the material
- spend all their time memorising it
- cannot answer questions that demand interpretation

Such shallow or surface learning encourages very poor learning skills and is not a good preparation for the complex interdependent demands of adult life.

Deep learning is when the student learns the material, not by rote, but by:

- absorbing it and synthesising it
- questioning it
- interpreting it

To Really Learn & Understand Something, You Must....

Read it...

Hear it....

SEE IT....

SAY IT...

& DO IT.

- seeing it from different angles
- utilising the holistic ways in which the mind actually works, like reading the material, discussing it, 'drawing' it in different forms, reciting it and really getting immersed in it or 'becoming' it

Artists and musicians talk in this transcendent way about their work, as do quantum physicists They are not remote from but really engaged with their material and it becomes a part of them. It is at this stage that learning becomes, in a way, transcendent, connecting the person to something bigger – in this case the whole subject and what it really means. In a way this is why we learn – so that we can relate to the complex universe that surrounds us, so that we can see ourselves in relationships to the bigger picture – life

THE STORY OF THE LOST BOY

Some fifteen years after the end of the Second World War a young Japanese boy was found in the jungle. He had been abandoned as an infant and brought up by monkeys. Totally cut off from the outside world, he'd never set eyes on another human being and was terribly limited in his interaction with his surroundings. Inevitably he had become fearful and withdrawn. Since he had not received any education as we know it, he had not really connected to the world in the way human beings can. He may have been doing really well by monkey standards but he was not interacting in a fully human way.

It is by understanding the world about us that we can begin to see our place and role in it. This is one of the main points of education: to use our incredibly complex brains to try to understand not only the incredibly complex universe outside us but also the incredibly complex world within us. This is the world of our emotions, feelings, talents, skills and creativity. This is why it is so important to learn how to learn.

If you really get to know how to learn deeply you will be able to take these skills with you into life, work and relationships. Education is not just about learning fractions or French or physics; it is rather how these subjects connect us to the outer and inner worlds.

7

COUNTDOWN TO JUDGEMENT DAY

THE DAY-TO-DAY SURVIVAL GUIDE FOR GETTING THROUGH YOUR EXAMS

This section is a guide to the rocky road through examinations. I have taken many students down that road and know it can be a hard one. Examinations *are* stressful, especially since they come at a stage in people's lives when they are vulnerable and inexperienced. It should be noted, though, that exam stress does not affect only the young.

A SOLDIER'S TALE

I remember once coaching a man in his mid-thirties in the NCEF. He was a former soldier who had served with the UN in the Lebanon and he was no wimp! During his practical exam, he had to teach an exercise session to a group. I happened to be the internal examiner and I noted that he became increasingly nervous and stressful as the exam progressed. By the end he was in a desperate state and only just got through it. During the break I asked him how he was. He smiled wryly. 'That was frightening,' he said. 'The last time I felt like that was on bomb-disposal duty in Lebanon, when I had to disarm a mortar shell.'

I tell that story to all my students for several reasons:

- It shows how frightening and stressful exams can be.
- It shows that age and experience can count for little.
- It shows that no matter how well you prepare there is always a risk in 'live' exams.

Too often I've seen well prepared, dedicated students fall to bits, while laid back, even lazy students do well. I emphasise to my students that exams are not a fair or real guide to people's performance but until we come up with a better system we have to play the game. Here I make available to you all the strategies, hints and advice I have absorbed over a decade of preparing students for national and international exams, both practical and written.

If you use these tips and combine them with note-mapping, six-step revision, deep learning and shared study-time I believe that you will not only succeed but do very well.

PHASE 1: THE PRE-MOCK PERIOD

Later we will look at this in detail. The main points are to

- look after your body
- eat well
- sleep well
- take exercise
- relax, reward your efforts and have fun when you've finished your tasks
- plan each day, using an A-list of 'have-tos and a B-list of 'like-tos
  As for study you should:
- map your notes
- revise lectures

- (i) within thirty minutes
- (ii) twenty-four hours later
- (iii) one week later
- (iv) one month later
- (v) before mocks
- (vi) before examination
- share study/revision with one or two friends
- seek sympathetic professional help if you become stuck

PHASE II: THE MOCK EXAMS –
'EVEN BETTER THAN THE REAL THING'

Use these to your advantage. Many people tend not to take advantage of the lessons they learn in the mocks. It's as if they can't bear to face failure. But wouldn't you rather hear the bad news now when things can be changed rather than when the results are final and everyone knows? I think it's vital to do your mocks under the same conditions as you do the actual exams. The more you can replicate the conditions the better.

When NASA is preparing its astronauts for the real thing they are made to go through countless simulations. These are contrived to be as close as possible to the stresses and strains of the real launch. In other words the astronauts go through countless mock exams and when the tests are over they spend many hours analysing and learning from the mistakes they made in their 'mocks'.

Try to do the same thing yourself. Try to remember exactly:

- how you feel during the mock exams
- how much tension you experience
- how much stress you suffer

Notice the small things which in the exam itself can become huge, such as how you feel:
- going to the exam
- sitting reading the papers
- planning your answers
- answering the questions
- experiencing common exam difficulties like writer's block, panic attacks and mind-blanking

You can learn from all these things and make changes before the big day. People do better if they really learn from their stress and exam anxieties, if they get to identify their fears and understand how they are affected by them. It is as if the fear is there for a reason (it is; it is there to help us avoid failing) and needs to be acknowledged. Once acknowledged, it will decrease and will probably not ruin your performance. I can sum up mock exams in a simple sentence: use your mocks or be mocked by them.

PHASE III: PERIOD BETWEEN MOCKS AND REAL EXAMS

This is perhaps the most critical part of your course. Put into practice all that you learnt from your mocks, especially your failures. Have a clear and manageable study plan that includes revision. Use the six-step revision plan. If you stick to it from the beginning you will need only to spend a few minutes on each topic you revise.

- Keep your notes in a clear mapped form that can easily be revised.
- Do not neglect to: eat well, sleep learn, exercise, relax and reward yourself. The tendency is to panic and work for too long as the exams approach. Remember: this strategy does not work.

- Keep your study periods to forty minutes maximum with ten-minute breaks.
- Use your friends and family to help you, test you and analyse how much you know. It is always easier if you share your work with others.
- Seek help if things seem to get out of control. For instance, you can write to me or arrange for me to give a *Maximum Points – Minimum Panic* revision day at your school or college.

PHASE IV: FOUR WEEKS TO GO

Talk to your teachers or tutors and get feedback on:

- your weaknesses
- your strengths
- what you should concentrate on
- questions they feel may come up

Don't forget to take an occasional morning or afternoon off as a reward. Go to the cinema, go fishing, get away from it all. You will be fresher and better able to do well as a result. Don't be influenced by panicking classmates; look after your own destiny. Surround yourself with people who are taking action, not panicking.

TWO WEEKS TO GO

Have a clear plan and know what you are going to concentrate on in these last days. Keep resting and listening to a relaxation and motivation tape like *Maximum Points – Minimum Panic* which will guide you through proven relaxation and learning exercises.

Use as much mental mapping and mental rehearsal as possible in dead time and study time. Remember you will be allowed to take only your 'head' into the exams – not your books.

ONE WEEK TO GO

The temptation will be to panic and cram. Resist it! They will only betray you. Keep to a well-organised plan, eat well and use the *Maximum Points* Minimum Panic tape to help you to rest. Take time for physical exercise and relaxation.

THREE DAYS TO GO

Spend time with friends and family revising and setting and answering tests in your head. Use books only to check answers. It is better to seek company now than be isolated, as isolation breeds fear of failure.

TWO DAYS TO GO

Everyone else will be 'boiling up'. But you, like a good prizefighter, should be winding down. By now it is too late to force-feed knowledge anyway. Blind panic, cramming and staying up late will only exhaust you.

Eat well, force yourself to take a walk, talk to friends, listen to your tape and keep the emphasis on mapping your revision, checking with your notes only after you have imagined the answers in your head.

ONE DAY TO GO

Study only for a final half-day, then in the afternoon do what footballers do before vital World Cup matches – go to the cinema (or do whatever relaxes you). By now all the work has been done or not done. If you have been following the advice in this book the unconscious will be ready. The biggest favour you can do yourself now is to rest.

TIREDNESS – A CATASTROPHIC TALE

What did the following disasters have in common: Chernobyl, Bhopal, Three-Mile Island and the *Exon Valdes*?

- They were all caused by human error due to overwork. All the personnel involved in these catastrophes had been working late at night during the period leading up to the disasters.
- They all occurred in the middle of the night. The enquiries set up to investigate these disasters all recommended that the workforce never again be forced to work long continuous shifts as this led directly to human error and the resulting disasters.

Are *you* working:
- long continuous hours?
- well into the night?

If so, you are becoming a walking disaster area. Take time off and rest before it is too late.

D-DAY CHECK LIST

In the days before D-day go through the following checklist:

- Check the time of your exams.
- Check the subject you will be examined on. This may sound obvious but each year several dozen people turn up in the wrong place at the wrong time for the wrong subject.
- Recheck your schedule for the next day, the subject, venue and time.
- Pack all your essential equipment: pens, rulers, pencils, compass, paper, erasers, crayons, watch or timer, special requirements e.g. dictionary, art materials, calculators where allowed.

- Pack soft drink, fruit or bar, chewing-gum, money, phone card.
- Pick the clothes you will wear – you need to be comfortable and dressed for the weather, not too hot or too cold.

LAST THING AT NIGHT BEFORE D-DAY

- Take a walk.
- Take a relaxing bath.
- Phone friends and wish them luck.
- Have a milky drink.
- Play your tape to help you to sleep.
- Say a prayer.

Now may be the appropriate time to thank the powers that keep us alive and well for minding us so far. Now is the time to let go and trust! As a human being you cannot do more than your best. After that it may be a good idea to let the universe unfold for you. It may also be a good time to thank your body and mind for serving you so well over the past months and years. Even though they have been tired they have worked loyally for you and your interests. Thanking them and telling them you will do your best to look after them over the coming exam days may feel right. You can really only ever give things your best shot. You deserve the best for what you have done and for what you are about to do as it requires courage and persistence. Sleep well and have happy dreams.

D-DAY

Just take a moment to reflect before you get up. You have worked long and hard. Now you are going to get up and give it your best shot. Take a few deep breaths and spend a few moments reflecting and gathering yourself before you get up into the hurly-burly. Eat something. You may feel sick but it is vital to take something. Blood sugar levels are low in the morning and you will not perform well on an empty stomach. Even Coca-Cola or an energy milk drink like Complan would be better than nothing. Check your kit before leaving or have someone read out your checklist for you as you go through all the items you're taking.

One Last Thing...
Research in America has shown that people are less likely to have an accident before lunch if they have a hug on leaving the house in the morning. So get or give a hug. If there are no humans about, hug the dog or cat. And if there are no pets hug your favourite teddy, computer game or U2 poster. Walk some of the way to the exam room. The exercise will clear your head and wake you up. Some people like to go to exams with a friend; others prefer solitude. Do what feels best for you.

Before Entering the Exam Centre
Try not to become too panicky and excited – certain classmates may be in this state and drain you of energy. If it feels right, stay on your own or with a friend going over some final map revision. Breathe normally. Play the *Maximum Points – Minimum Panic* tape on your Walkman to relax you and put you in the right frame of mind. Keep focused on what you are about to do. Save energy.

On Entering the Exam Room
Find your desk. Don't rush; no one else is going to sit there. Set out your pens, pencils, etc. and sit just taking in the room: how it feels, what the atmosphere is like. Locate the

toilets and clock. Listen carefully to the invigilator, the person who will supervise your exam. Note down any instructions he may issue. Ask him to repeat if you can't hear him.

STARTING YOUR EXAM

Set your watch and turn over the paper. Remember that relevant studies suggest three main reasons for failing written exams:

1. Students do not read questions: they answer questions that are not asked.
2. Students spend too much time answering one question.
3. Students do not answer all questions; they don't finish the paper.

Let us spend a little time on each of these points and devise simple guidelines:

1 CANDIDATES DO NOT READ QUESTION

Spend at least two minutes reading the question before you pick up your pen. Examiners spend hours deciding on the form of the question. When we put together questions for the NCEF exams my group of tutors spend a couple of hours checking that the questions make sense and can be easily interpreted. The questions are then vetted by the NCEF exam committee at the University of Limerick. Nothing is left to chance. It will be the same with your exam questions. They are designed with a clear answer in mind. It is your job to find the answer and not come out with the first thing that rushes into your head.

So spend the two minutes looking for the answers

the examiners want. If you have been study-sharing and designing exam questions to test your classmates you will have no problems with this as you will already know what it is like to be an examiner.

2 CANDIDATES SPEND TOO MUCH TIME ANSWERING ONE QUESTION

Examinations are usually marked out of 100. Each question is worth a certain number of marks and should be answered in a corresponding time frame. Learn that time and never go beyond it. If you do you will:

- lose marks on other, unanswered, questions
- waste time – you can only get the set marks no matter how long you spend on one question
- put yourself under extreme stress as you see time running out

3 CANDIDATES DON'T ANSWER ALL THE QUESTIONS

Again it is a matter of simple arithmetic. Let's say the pass mark is 60 per cent, as it is on the NCEF written paper. Let's say you answer only seven questions at eight marks each. That's fifty-six marks – a fail! Tragically this does happen. I have been a member of the NCEF examination review board which sits to decide students' final results and I have noticed how students who obviously know their stuff fail by not completing their papers. An average student who gets only the basic pass mark of six but completes all ten questions often does better than the excellent student who does not answer all questions. *It is essential to complete all questions.*

If you have made a reasonable shot at all the questions you will almost certainly get at least a pass mark. If you attempt only half the questions, you cannot pass, however well you answer them.

The common wisdom is to start with the easy questions and go on from there. By the time you have answered a couple of these you will be warmed up, in your flow and able to tackle the harder ones. You may also want to leave an easy question for last – as you may be under time pressure.

READ EACH QUESTION CAREFULLY AND MAKE A PLAN

Put down your pen and let the question sink in for a couple of minutes. Decide what the examiners want. Then check that against the question again. Only when you are sure you are on the right lines, say after two to three minutes, should you jot down your plan for the answer. Use simple key words and bullet points. For example, let's go back to our rain forest lecture. Just spend a moment recalling your map. See it in your mind. Now let's see how you'd plan an answer to the following question. 'Describe the environmental dangers that result from the destruction of the Brazilian rain forest.' Jot down your bullet points. Now compare them with my examiner's answer below. Remember when examiners set questions they also have to provide the model answer which the markers will use to judge if you have answered the question correctly. My examiner's answer would be:

- *loss of flora*, impact on medicine, research and future cures
- *loss of fauna*, extinction threatens global gene pool
- *loss of global lung* that clears air and stabilises global warming
- *loss of the native tribe*, another irreplaceable environ-

mental loss
- *loss of natural land*, the size of Wales, every year
- conclusion – how this all adds up to a real threat to our environment

NOW WRITE THE ANSWER, CAREFULLY FOLLOWING YOUR PLAN

Examiners want answers clearly argued and written so:
- do not deviate from your plan
- keep the answer short and to the point
- write as clearly as possible
- finish answers on time.

Check with your tutor in advance whether the examiners want to see your plan. If so, write it down so they will be able to see your intentions. It will help if you don't have time to finish the question.

TO RECAPITULATE – EXAM GUIDELINES

- Read instructions.
- Read paper through.
- Select your questions.
- Read each question and think about it for 1-2 minutes.
- Write out plan.
- Write answer from plan in right amount of time.
- Answer all questions.
- Write clearly and simply.

If you do this it will be difficult to fail.

AFTER THE EXAMS

Discuss the exam with friends but beware of going into a decline. Our exam culture produces paranoia, especially at exam times. On the NCEF and ITEC courses I teach I spend a huge amount of time reassuring students who have made some small omission or mistake. Be realistic – you will make at least one mistake, probably more, in every exam you do. It does not mean you have failed or even done badly – it just means you're human. Give yourself a break – the exams are tough enough without your beating yourself up.

Reward Yourself
After the first hurdle – don't burn yourself out by worrying over something that's done. You can't bring it back. If you do feel bad, find a friend or a quiet place and acknowledge that feeling of having let yourself down – it is there only to protect you from failure. Honour it and it will eventually quieten down.

Now take a break, reward yourself. You've done well. Keep your energy up as there are more exams and pressure to come.

TIPS FOR THE REST OF THE EXAMS

Avoid going into 'panic mode' as so many people around you will have done. Keep:

- exercising
- eating well
- using the sleep tape
- taking sometime out to walk and relax
- study-sharing and using maps as the basis of revision with friends

It may not mean much to you at this point, but exams are not the end of the world. Give them your best shot – it's all you can do and it's enough. Avoid coffee, sugary snacks and cigarettes or alcohol – at least until the exams over. These will only hype you up and your job now is to:

- stay focused
- stay cool
- stay with the 'now'. The past is gone, the future has not yet arrived.

  Keep a daily check on:
- when your next exam is
- what it is
- what time it's on
- what special requirements it has

- Above all remember you are only human and human beings:
- get stressed
- get pessimistic
- get tired
- get anxious
- make mistakes

You can turn all these things around. Remember, during this whole process there is only one thing you can do – your best.

8

IS THERE LIFE AFTER EXAMS?

I was talking recently to an eminent professor and poet who teaches first years at university. He made an interesting point that every year his class was full of fresh-faced first years who were 'mark obsessed'. They all judged one another on how well they had done in their exams. This was all-important – and not what sort of people they were or what their dreams or aspirations were. This is the 'points culture', getting value exclusively from how well you have done in exams. Perhaps you do not want to get locked into that way of thinking; perhaps you don't look at life in that way at all. I hope not. This final chapter is aimed at looking beyond the exams culture and seeing:

- what's out there for me in life
- what do I want
- what can I contribute to life
- where do I want to go from here

After exams and after college we all face the real world. Wouldn't it be great if we could make choices about our life that are informed and real, corresponding to our own unique personalities? Consider the following marvellous things about you:

- You are completely a 'one off' – never to be repeated.
- It's taken 4,000 billion years of evolution to bring you about.
- You will not, in your present form, come back to this planet for a second chance.

This is your big chance to do something, make your own unique contribution. As they say, 'This is not a rehearsal – this is the real thing!' So what do you want and where do you want to go?

WHOSE LIFE IS IT ANYWAY?

You will never be short of people who will want to live life for you. They know best what you should and should not do. They would be quite happy to have you as a carbon copy of themselves to live out the ambitions they never could achieve themselves. Beware of these influences. They can make your life very frustrating and difficult. They can actually stop you being yourself

Look at the list below and take a moment to see if the influence people exert on you is positive or negative. By positive I mean:

- inspiring
- giving guidance while leaving freedom of choice
- giving advice while knowing you may not always follow it
- helping you become the unique person you really are

By negative I mean:

- controlling

- manipulating
- using fear or guilt or emotional blackmail to make you toe the line
- making you into their image and not your own

WHAT SORT OF INFLUENCE DO PEOPLE EXERT ON ME?

Think for a moment about what sort of influence: positive, negative or mixed?

People	Positive	Negative	Mixed
Mother			
Father			
Brothers and sisters			
Close family members			
Church			
Teachers			
Neighbourhood and social group			
Peer pressure – what friends think			
Pressure through advertising			
Media			

Then there are the special influences that society imposes on you in the matter of drugs, alcohol, gender, man/woman stereotypes, sex. Only after you have worked through these pressures and influences will you truly become an individual.

FEELING RIGHT ABOUT THINGS IN YOUR LIFE

I can know what is right for me because it feels right in the core of my being, in a place that is somehow free of prejudice and influence and ambition.

Mystics throughout time have known this place, poets have praised it and priests of all religions have preached it. The psychologist Jung referred to the 'inner wisdom' of the body, the feeling that is beyond ambition, joining us to a bigger wisdom, a collective unconscious or knowing. It is the small quiet voice of conscience, that comes to us in peaceful moments, in sudden insights, in intuitions.

It's the voice that often offers us a harder choice in life but it is the voice we ignore at our peril. Take time out to listen to that 'small quiet voice' and see:

- how it feels when you follow its direction or plan
- how you feel when you go against it's direction or plan

If it feels bad when you go against it, it is probably the right voice.

HOW CAN I KNOW WHAT I WANT TO BE IN LIFE?

A simple way is to put aside all the pressure exerted by others and ask this question: 'If I were guaranteed success in whatever I choose to do what would that be?' Give yourself time to answer that question. You will come up against a thousand 'can'ts' and 'shouldn'ts' but let yourself go beyond that; let your imagination soar. You will eventually find what you want to do, if not now then later. Then it's up to you to decide if you want to exert the effort and run the necessary risks to pursue it.

I have found that this is a question that can have a profound effect on people, whether they're fourteen or sixty-four. After seminars in which we ask this question I have had the experience of people getting in touch with me months later to say that they had taken the first step

WHERE AM I GOING IN LIFE?
THE ROAD TO THE future....

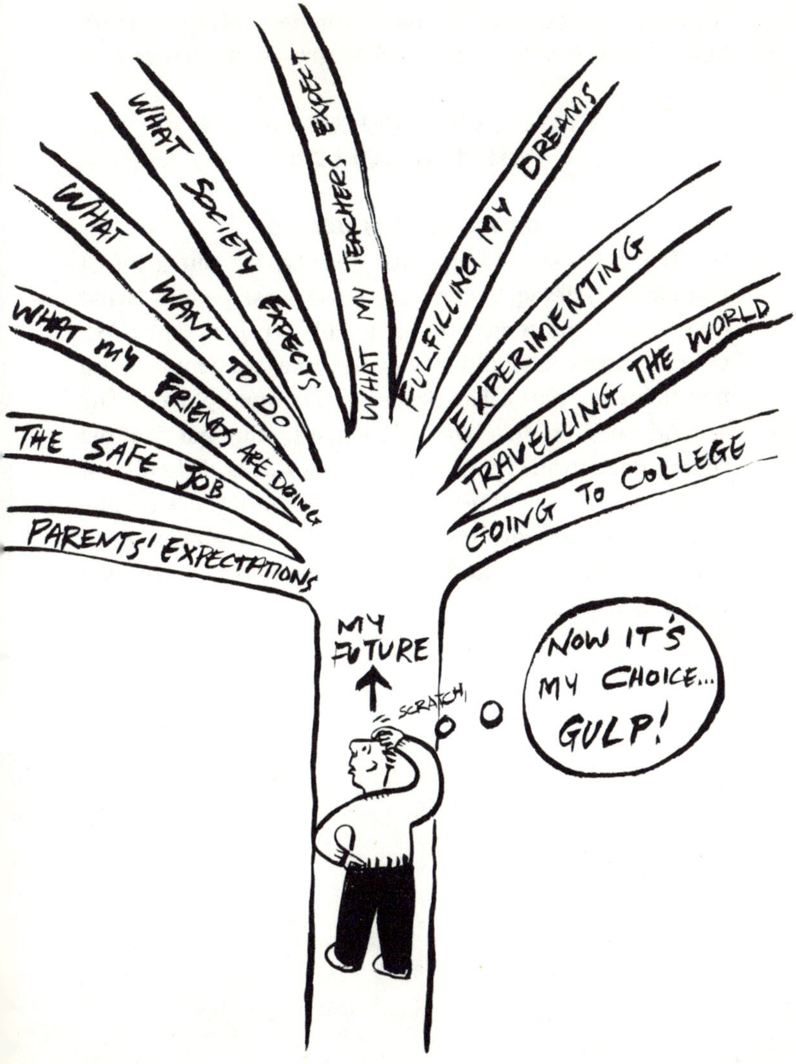

to achieving a long-held dream and that they felt so much better for taking that step.

When answering this question fill in the cartoon below with an image of yourself fulfilling that dream. By drawing, you use the right side of the brain as well as the left and it really makes you think of your dream in a different, more holistic way. Try it – you may be surprised at what comes.

IF I WERE GUARANTEED SUCCESS WHAT WOULD I DO?

BEING VERSUS DOING

We live in a very materialistic society. We put a lot of emphasis on doing. In conversations we ask people, 'What do you do?' and tend to judge people on their reply. Ask yourself how you would feel about these two people if you met them at a party. The first says: 'I'm unemployed.' The second says: 'I'm in a band and we're signing our first big record deal.' Notice how you react, how it is difficult not to downgrade one and romanticise the other. It's human nature to a degree but our society also places great emphasis on what you do and less on who you are. Just check your own life.

If I was Guaranteed Success in Whatever I Chose to do in Life, What would I do?

DRAW A PICTURE OF YOU DOING WHAT YOU REALLY WANT TO DO IN LIFE.

WHAT MAKES ME VALUABLE?

	Agree	Disagree
The amount of money I have		
The school I go to		
The college I will go to		
The area I live in		
The jobs my parents have		
The sort of jeans I wear		
The car I will drive		
The job I'll have		

OR IS IT THESE THINGS THAT MAKE ME VALUABLE?

	Agree	Disagree
How much I respect myself and others		
How much time I take to listen to others		
How much time I take to help others, especially those who haven't 'made it'		
How much time I take, if any, caring for:		
the environment I live in		
my fellow human beings		
my family		
my friends		
my body		
my soul		

In the end, of course, it is not simple. Life is a combination of the material and metaphysical, or body and soul. The problem arises when we become preoccupied with one area to the exclusion of another. A really valuable question to ask yourself is: 'Why am I valuable?' If you ask yourself that often enough you will get challenging answers.

Finally it's all down to the question that has dominated human thinking from the beginning:

WHY AM I HERE?

I hope that this book will prompt you just a little to find your own unique answer to this question. In the end perhaps that's what the whole education system is about, discovering our place in this amazing world. In the great scheme of things passing exams is just one small part of life. I feel strongly that no one should ever feel so badly about exams that they suffer trauma and mental turmoil or even despair. Unfortunately the pressures are growing and more people are succumbing to them. It is time that we, as a society, seriously considered what we are doing to our own young adults.

Finally I will leave you with a few more ideas to help you look at your own future beyond exams. You can come back and try them at any time during your life – they will always have something important to say.

THE 100-YEAR QUESTION

When you're stressed about something and driving yourself crazy, just ask yourself: 'Will this matter in 100 years time?' and wait for the reply. You will be amazed at what comes.

THE TOMBSTONE QUESTION

Not really a depressing exercise but one that can put things in perspective. First fill in how you would like to be remembered. Then draw another tombstone and write down what people would say about you if you happened to die right now. This can be a very enlightening exercise as the two may radically differ. Which one is right? Try it and see.

WHAT MARK WILL I LEAVE ON THE EARTH?

We all leave a mark on the world, big or small. Ask yourself the question: 'Will I leave a scorch mark, a presence on the planet so that in some way things are worse than before I arrived?' Or 'Will I leave a green shoot that may grow into a plant or tree and feed or shelter further generations?'

LEAVING OUR IMPRESSION

It's been said that the only thing we really leave behind us is our impression on the people we have somehow touched. It can be good to ask ourselves how we have so far touched those around us. How have we affected our:

- mother
- father
- sisters
- brothers
- friends
- neighbours
- school mates
- work mates
- loved ones
- animals
- pets
- plants
- earth
- anything else we may have touched

Think for a moment about each and then answer to yourself.

Finally, it's been said that the exam or points system may be the first step of the rat race. I remind you of the words of Hollywood actress Lily Tomlin: 'So what if you win the rat race – you're still only a rat'.

At the end of it all – you are not a rat but a unique, precious miracle. May all your efforts to find your own true, remarkable self be successful. I wish you luck in this, the only real exam that counts.

FURTHER READING

If you are interested in any of the subjects touched on in this book and wish to pursue them you may find the following selection of titles of interest. They also contain further details of the various research studies mentioned in the book.

Chopra, Deepak. *Quantum Healing.* Bantam Press, 1989.
(Medical research on the impact of emotions and stress on health)

Dossey, Larry. *Healing Words.* Harper Collins, 1993.
(Fascinating research on the science of healing, prayer and thinking)

Gendlin, Eugene. *Focusing.* Bantam Press, 1981.
(The ground-breaking book on the process mentioned above)

Goleman, Daniel. *Emotional Intelligence.* Bantam Press, 1995.
(Amazing research on the functions of the brain and feeling)

Siegel, Bernie. *Love, Medicine and Miracles.* Rider, 1986.
(Research on the mind and body link)

FURTHER INFORMATION

This book is available in all bookshops or may be ordered direct from Mercier Bookshop, PO Box 5, 5 French Church Street, Cork. Price £6.99 including packing and postage. All major credit cards accepted. The *Maximum Points – Minimum Panic* audio tape is available from the author, Kevin Flanagan, at The Stress Clinic, 13 Fitzwilliam Street Upper, Dublin 2. Price £6.99 (incl. p.&p.).

If you would like more information on the areas specified, please photocopy this form, fill in and return to Kevin Flanagan at the above address.

☐ *Maximum Points – Minimum Panic* audio tape
☐ Kevin's 1-day school or college workshops
☐ Kevin's focusing workshops

Name _____

Address _____

_____

_____

Telephone _____

Fax _____

e-mail _____

REPEAT STRESS TEST

HOW STRESSED AM I?

Directions

You have put into practice the guidelines outlined in this book and given them time to work. Now fill in this 'repeat' stress chart and see if there is a difference. Put a cross where you think you are on the graph. Don't think about it too long. Then join up the xs.

BODY

Relaxed	0 1 2 4 5 6 7 8 9 10	Extreme Stress
Steady heartbeat	. . . .	Palpitations
Calm relaxed feelings	. . . .	'On edge' feelings
Dry hands and brow	. . . .	Clammy hands and brow
Slow steady breathing	. . . .	Fast breathing, shortness of breath
Steady hand, relaxed muscles	. . . .	Shaking hand, tensed muscles, stiff neck or shoulders
Steady flow of energy; don't get tired easily	. . . .	Sudden 'bursts' of frantic energy followed by exhaustion, extreme tiredness
Sleep like a log	. . . .	Can't sleep at all
Eat well regularly	. . . .	Can't eat at all or binge
Digest food easily	. . . .	Can't digest food at all
Skin, hair and eyes bright and healthy	. . . .	Skin, hair and eyes dull or blotchy

MIND

Relaxed	0 1 2 4 5 6 7 8 9 10	Extreme Stress
Can make decisions and stick with them	. . . .	Can't make decisions or keep changing mind
Can calculate and see all sides of a problem	. . . .	Can't calculate or see what the problem is at all
Can work long hours doing 'brain' work	. . . .	Can't do any 'brain' work at all

EMOTIONS

Relaxed	0 1 2 4 5 6 7 8 9 10	Extreme Stress
Steady, reliable mood	. . . .	Extreme mood swings
Sense of feeling 'good' about life	. . . .	Depression or feeling 'bad' about life
Feeling 'I can cope'	. . . .	Feeling 'I can't cope'
Feeling loved by family	. . . .	Feeling unloved by family
Feeling supported by friends	. . . .	Feeling 'I have no friends'

SOUL

Relaxed	0 1 2 4 5 6 7 8 9 10	**Extreme Stress**
Feeling I'm worth a lot	. . . .	Feeling I'm worth nothing
Feeling life is definitely worth living	. . . .	Feeling life is not worth living
Feeling I am loved by people and/or a higher power	. . . .	Feeling unloved by people and/or a higher power
Feeling my life has a a purpose	. . . .	Feeling my life is purposeless
Feeling there is love and protection in the world	. . . .	Feeling threatened and vulnerable
Feeling I have a part to play in life	. . . .	Feeling I have no part part to play in life at all